the CHRISTIAN ENTREPRENEUR

the CHRISTIAN

ENTREPRENEUR

Carl Kreider

Foreword by Willard M. Swartley

HERALD PRESS
Scottdale, Pennsylvania
Kitchener, Ontario
1980

Library of Congress Cataloging in Publication Data

Kreider, Carl Jonas, 1914-
    The Christian entrepreneur.

    (The Conrad Grebel lectures; 1979)
    Includes bibliographical references and index.
    1. Christian life—Mennonite authors.
2. Business—Moral and religious aspects—Mennonites
3. Christian giving. I. Title. II. Series:
Conrad Grebel lectures; 1979.
BV4501.2.K72   248.4'897   80-16836
ISBN 0-8361-1936-3 (pbk.)

THE CHRISTIAN ENTREPRENEUR
Copyright © 1980 by Herald Press, Scottdale, Pa. 15683
    Published simultaneously in Canada by Herald Press,
    Kitchener, Ont. N2G 4M5
Library of Congress Catalog Card Number: 80-16836
International Standard Book Number: 0-8361-1936-3
Printed in the United States of America
Design: Alice B. Shetler

15 14 13 12 11 10 9 8 7 6 5 4 3 2 1

To men and women who
use their business skills
to serve Christ

Contents

Foreword

Today's religious book market is flooded with Christian discussion of sex, family life, devotional life, aging, coping with stress, end-times prognostications, and on goes the list. But where are the books addressed to the Christian's use of money, Christian morality in business, and financial accountability to God? Writings in this field are alarmingly meager.

Jesus spoke many times more often about economic matters than he did about prayer. Books, sermons, sharing groups, and retreats of all kinds speak to the importance of prayer in the Christian life. But where in the church today do we hear clear teaching on economic issues?

To be faithful to Jesus we must recover the gospel's concern for our everyday economic decisions. What moral admonition and theological perspectives does the Bible provide for Christian men and women in business today?

Because this book speaks to this urgent question in a va-

riety of specific and helpful ways, I am happy to commend it
for your reading, pondering, and practical response.

Carl Kreider's outstanding service to Goshen College
through the years, both as an esteemed teacher of economics
and an able administrator as dean of a church college,
provides a rare blend of qualifications for writing this book.
The chapters that follow reflect the wisdom of an informed
economist and the commitment of a dedicated churchman.

Assuming that Christians live within economic systems,
capitalism in the case of his readers, the author identifies numerous points where the Christian entrepreneur must make
decisions which reflect the values and priorities of his or her
kingdom loyalties. These decisions, rooted in biblical teaching, embrace basic issues, such as whether a Christian employer has a right to a higher standard of living than the
lower paid employees. Or, how much money should a Christian entrepreneur spend on vacations? Or, what guidelines
and plan (and Kreider suggests some) should Christian business people follow in determining how much money should
be kept for self or family and how much should be given
away?

This book merits serious study and practical response
from all Christians in business. It should be discussed in
small groups in church congregations in order to assist all
God's people to do right in this arena of life sorely needing a
"watchman on the wall."

With gratitude to Carl Kreider and on behalf of the
Conrad Grebel Projects Committee, I heartily commend this
book.

Willard M. Swartley
Executive Secretary,
Conrad Grebel Projects Committee

Author's Preface

This book is written primarily for Christians engaged in business. It speaks of ethical problems these people face. I hope that the comments I make may be of some interest to students of ethics, but it hasn't been written primarily with the specialist in ethics in mind. It makes many biblical references; though it hasn't been written primarily for biblical scholars, I would be pleased if they would find it helpful. Many of the questions on which I speak have their roots in economic issues, but in writing it I did not have the professional economist in mind. Rather my target audience is the rapidly increasing number of Christians engaged in business—people who want to be faithful to Christ their Lord, people who want to be responsibly functioning members of the body of Christ, the church, but people whose occupations place them in an increasingly competitive and increasingly secular business world.

Entrepreneurs are persons who organize, manage, and

bear the financial risks of business enterprises. In this work they exercise considerable initiative and assume substantial risks. I have written this book to help people who are pursuing these entrepreneurial functions.

Sometimes Christians who engage in business have wondered whether they are accepted as "full-fledged" members of the church. The idea that business is dirty has a long history. During the Middle Ages the "Christian attitude toward commerce . . . was one of active antagonism." St. Augustine held, " 'Business is in itself an evil,' that profit . . . was avarice, that to make money out of money by charging interest on a loan was the sin of usury, that buying goods wholesale and selling them unchanged at a higher retail price was immoral . . . that, in short, St. Jerome's dictum was final, 'A man who is a merchant can seldom if ever please God.' "[1] I have written this book in the confidence that Christian entrepreneurs can "please God" and can function as an integral part of the body of Christ.

I could have entitled the book "The Christian Businessman" but that would suggest a sexual bias for some of my readers. From earliest times both women and men have been engaged in business, though in most societies more men than women have been so engaged.[2] But many wives have been intimately involved in business decisions; sometimes they have taken the dominant position and have had greater business sense than their husbands. When I visited Poland a few years ago I found that many of the small, privately owned farms were managed by women. I was informed that this has a long history—that women needed to manage the farms when their husbands were called away to engage in war. Today they manage the farm because their husbands are bussed daily to urban districts to serve as factory or construction workers.

I could have entitled the book "The Christian Business Person" but frankly I find that a clumsy way to avoid a sexist title. Instead I have used the perhaps unfamiliar word entrepreneur, a word which refers to function rather than to the sex of the person engaging in the function. An entrepreneur may be a man, a woman, or both jointly. But in the text of the book for the sake of literary variety I will sometimes refer to these people as entrepreneurs, sometimes as business people, and sometimes as businessmen or businesswomen. If I say "businessman" I use man in the same generic sense that has been used through the ages in referring to "mankind."

This book was commissioned by the Conrad Grebel Projects Committee of the Mennonite Board of Education. I served on this committee for many years and was on the committee when the book was first suggested. Its completion was delayed partly because my return to full-time teaching has proved to be a demanding occupation after spending years as a college administrator with only marginal time available for teaching. A chronic physical illness left me with a lower energy level than I formerly enjoyed. But most important of all, the delay was a result of the fact that I wanted to write the most helpful book possible and I wasn't completely sure what to say. Though I now write with apparent confidence I must confess that I am still not sure of the correctness of all of the judgments I make. I concluded that I could never be sure, and if I waited for this certainty the book would never be written. And so the book is intended to stimulate dialogue and through this process yield practical conclusions which are more valid than my initial, tentative statements.

I have thought many years about the questions raised by this book. I have often talked about them with my students in college classes and in Sunday school classes. But one doesn't have to be as precise when thinking or talking as when writing. There is a real value in writing down your thoughts—especially if you are aware that someone else may read them and perhaps disagree with you. Furthermore, if you write an idea down you may return to it later on to modify it, expand it, or clarify it.[3] If you disagree with me, write your disagreements. Formulate your own ideas on this subject and state them the way you think they should be said. This will help you in your own thinking and in subsequent discussions you may have with other members of the business community who are your Christian friends. I would also be delighted if you would write your comments in a personal letter to me.

Some of my most committed Christian friends will probably be disappointed with the position taken by this book. They feel, as the editor of *Sojourners* expressed it, that "the lesson of Acts 2 is that any spiritual renewal that doesn't result in a new political economy is an incomplete, if not an inauthentic, spirituality."[4] I am not sure whether the "new political economy" he envisages is a national economy such as Christian socialists have long advocated or small Christian communal groups within a larger capitalistic order which stand in contrast to and in judgment on the larger order. I presume he means the latter.

I have the highest regard for intentional communities that are built on a firmly Christian base. They are a splendid illustration of Christian nonconformity in economic affairs. But the Bible clearly teaches that they were not the *only* form of economic organization practiced by members of the early church. I believe that the position I have taken in this book is also a radical form of economic nonconformity. I hope that my friends who believe that Acts 2 is the only "authentic" form of Christian community will give serious consideration to the demands which the alternative presented by this book requires. This alternative, like that of Christian communalism, has deep biblical roots.

I want to thank the Conrad Grebel Projects Committee for making this book possible. I want to thank those who have heard me give the lectures in whole or in part for their comments and criticisms. I am especially grateful to the advisory committee who read an initial draft of the book and who made many helpful suggestions. Those persons were Arthur DeFehr of Winnipeg, Manitoba; Ben Cutrell and Ralph Hernley of Scottdale, Pennsylvania; and Roy Mullet of Hesston, Kansas. Willard Swartley, executive secretary of the Conrad Grebel Projects Committee, and Tilman R. Smith, past member of the Projects Committee, also read the entire manuscript and made many helpful comments. Arthur DeFehr was the most critical of all of the readers of the first draft of this book. His background includes an amazing combination of top-level graduate study in business administration, leadership in a business enterprise, and a compassion stemming in part from MCC service in Bangladesh. He made comments on nearly every page—comments which I always took seriously even though I did not always agree with them.

My son, Alan F. Kreider, read the initial manuscript with great care, made dozens of incisive comments, and helped me improve my style of writing. He confirmed what some other readers had also suggested, namely that I should add to my book what has since become chapter seven. My wife, Evelyn Burkholder Kreider, gave me much encouragement and supporting love. She had hoped that when I retired from college administration I might be satisfied with a five-day working week. When I decided to write this book she accepted with her usual good grace the shattering of that hope.

I gave public lectures at Goshen College, Eastern Mennonite College, and Hesston College in April 1979 based on parts of this book. I have benefited much from the discussions following these public lectures. Sometimes those who read my manuscript or heard my lectures gave conflicting advice. In all cases I knew that I would finally be held responsible. Therefore, if you don't like what I say, blame me, not the advisory committee members. If, on the other hand, you find my writing helpful, give God the glory. I have written it with the confidence that he will smile indulgently when he knows that I am wrong and my critics are right.

Carl Kreider
Goshen College
Goshen, Indiana
August 1979

the CHRISTIAN ENTREPRENEUR

CHAPTER 1

Introduction

The enormous increase in production is one of the amazing features of the past 200 years. Historians sometimes refer to the events which sparked this increase as the Industrial Revolution. The production of goods which heretofore was carried on primarily in the home or artisan's shop in the village now shifted to the factory. As the Industrial Revolution advanced these factories became larger and larger. Whereas in 1776 Adam Smith,[1] the father of modern economics, did not even think of the business corporation as being involved in manufacturing enterprises, today 85 percent of the receipts of all business enterprises go to corporations. We scarcely think of manufacturing apart from the large-scale business corporation.

Production: The Creation of Utility

The economist speaks of production as the "creation of utility." But that doesn't help much until we define utility.

Utility is simply the capacity of a thing to satisfy a human want. It is sometimes subdivided into: (1) form utility, (2) place utility, (3) time utility, and (4) ownership utility. Manufacturing is essentially the creation of *form utility*. The automobile has more utility than the steel, aluminum, copper, rubber, and plastics which have been combined in its production. Because of this greater utility we are willing to pay more for the finished automobile than we would for the sum of its component parts. The transportation industry creates *place utility*. Strawberries have a greater utility as they provide a dessert for my meal than they do in the strawberry patch on the farm. Those who pick and transport the berries from the patch to my table are creating place utility. In the northern hemisphere apples sell for a higher price in the spring than in the harvest time in the fall. This means that storage facilities have produced *time utility*. Finally, we are willing to pay a broker a fee for selling our house because he has engaged in the productive act of finding a buyer who judges that (for him) our house has a higher utility than it does for us (the seller). In other words, the broker has rendered the productive service of creating *ownership utility*.

Now it should be noted that the economist does not pass an ethical judgment on the utility which has been created. Instead, the measurement of utility is a purely monetary one. If the automobile sells for $2,000 more than materials from which the automobile was made, we say that the manufacturer has created $2,000 worth of form utility. But because utility is the capacity of a thing to satisfy a human want, and because wants may be dominated by sinful desires rather than legitimate needs, there will always be things which for Christians have no usefulness and yet which may command a high price in the market. Mink coats are an example of this. But there are many others, some of which may satisfy more clearly legitimate needs than others. In other words the ultimate "usefulness" of goods and services from an ethical rather than an economic standard is open to debate.

It is always well for us to remember this amoral nature of economics. The ultimate measure of the economic value of any good produced or service rendered is the marketplace. Things and services are "worth" what people are willing to pay for them—whether they are really good, indifferent, or harmful. Obviously, this means that as Christians we won't be satisfied with mere economic considerations. I will say more about this later.

Alongside the Industrial Revolution mentioned earlier, agrarian and commercial revolutions were taking place. The agrarian revolution enabled the United States, Canada, western Europe, and Japan to increase enormously their output of agricultural products. At the same time the proportion of the population engaged in agriculture in the United States declined from over 90 percent in colonial times to less than 4 percent today. The commercial revolution resulted in an amazing expansion of transportation, communications, and financial institutions. The Industrial Revolution, the agrarian revolution, and the commercial revolution have all served to make the modern age the most productive era in human history.

Factors of Production: Land, Labor, and Capital

In a modern economy goods and services are produced from land, labor, and capital. By land I mean all God-given natural resources. This includes the soil we use to grow our crops, minerals, natural waterways, harbors, and even climatic conditions which are favorable to production. Land with adequate rainfall (enough but not too much), suitably spread over the growing season, is superior to desert land or to water-logged swamps. But even deserts can be tremendously productive if, as in the Middle East, they have enormous reserves of oil beneath the surface.

By labor I mean any productive work done by human beings. Of course this includes the large number of people who work with their hands—the "laborers" as we refer to them. But it also includes those who work with their minds—the decision makers and the thinkers; or those who work with their voices and their minds—the public speakers, teachers, singers. Any one who renders a service which has utility (that satisfies someone's want) is a member of the labor force.

Capital is usually defined as "produced means of production." It arises because someone has felt that it will make his/her work more productive. It inevitably involves *saving*. It stems from a decision to forgo the direct production of some consumer good in order to allow time to produce some (capital) good which will hopefully increase the production of consumer goods in the future. When a primitive man made a simple plow from a piece of wood he was engaged in the production of capital. But while he was producing capital he was not satisfying his immediate need for food. He "saved" (abstained from consumption) in order that he might have more food (greater consumption) later on after he had produced his capital (plow).

Modern production is becoming more and more capitalistic. This is true not only in the capitalistic societies of North America, Western Europe, and Japan but in the socialistic or communistic countries of eastern Europe and China. In fact, one of the major devices these countries used to make their economies more productive was to give a higher priority to the production of capital goods than consumer goods. The lesser-developed economies of the Third World are also planning increased emphasis on capital formation.

The Entrepreneur: A Factor of Production

Land, labor, and capital have all contributed to the enormous expansion of production. But this book is about another factor of production: the entrepreneur. This word is a French word which we might translate as "undertaker."[2] But since "undertaker" in English usually means a funeral director or mortician, it might be better to translate it "enterpriser." But the French word is clearly established in the English language and I prefer to use it. The entrepreneur is the one who bears the *risks* of a business enterprise. It is this risk-bearing function that differentiates the entrepreneur from the laborer. Thus the highly skilled manager of a business enterprise who bears no risks is a laborer rather than an entrepreneur. But executive compensation plans involving bonuses or profit-sharing seek to combine the entrepreneurial and the labor functions.

The entrepreneur has to decide what combinations of land, labor, and capital he/she will use in the productive process. Usually the decision will be made by a careful calculation of the relative costs of the various factors of production. At other times decisions may be based more on intuition.

The farmer owner-operator is clearly an entrepreneur. Let us assume that he has a small farm and that he is not satisfied with the income he is receiving from the farm. In the terms I have been using, he is not satisfied with the farm's productivity. He could produce more if he increased any one or any combination of the three factors of production. He might buy or rent more land. If so, he is increasing the use of land as a factor of production. He might tile the land, fence it in from predators, add fertilizer to it, buy farm tools or machinery, or in other ways increase the amount of capital he employs in the productive process. Or he might hire additional workers and thus use more labor in the productive process. He might use the land more intensively—changing a pasture, for instance, into a vegetable garden. Or he might go to a long-term investment and change the pastureland into a fruit orchard. Or he might subdivide the land into plots for building sites for homes or factories.

Whatever the decision the farmer makes in this matter will almost certainly involve the expenditure of additional money. He decides to spend more money for much the same reasons as the primitive man stopped producing food long enough to make a rudimentary plow: he thinks that his income will be increased. But he has no absolute assurance of this. There is clearly an element of risk involved. The costs of the added input (more land, labor, or capital) may be greater than the added output (increase in production). If so he will be worse off than before. Or he may make an error in judgment as to the kind of input he is adding. He may be hiring an additional worker (more labor) when he should have bought a tractor (more capital). He may buy more land when he should farm more intensively the land he already owns. This risk-bearing function of the entrepreneur is just as important and necessary a part of the productive process as the use of land, labor, and capital. The economic reward for successfully bearing this risk function is *profit*. The penalty for taking unwise risks is *loss*.

My illustration has been taken from the small-scale farmer. I am assuming that the form of business enterprise he uses is that of the sole proprietorship. In this business form one person is the owner; this person is ultimately responsible for all of the business decisions, including the risk of debts. He may do most of the work himself, or he may hire others to do all or part of it. Larger businesses are sometimes partnerships where the ownership costs and the managerial responsibilities are shared by two or more people. Or the business may be a corporation, which receives a charter from the state or province and in which the owners are the stockholders. Whatever the form the business takes it is the owner (or owners) who receives the profit if the entrepreneurial decisions have been wisely made; the owner (or owners) suffers the losses if the decisions have been wrong. The owners are the risk bearers.

Profits and Losses

Profit is not necessarily the same as net income. In the sole proprietorship the net income is the bottom line of the income statement. It consists of gross receipts minus the expenses. It is a figure similar to the "adjusted gross income" of the Federal income tax statement. But such net income is really a combination of labor income (wages), land income (rent), and capital income (interest).

In a proprietorship or partnership all three of these may be implicit rather than explicit. No actual money transfers may be involved. For example, if the farmer owns his land and farm machinery and buildings and does his own work, his net income should be enough to give him a fair wage for his work, a rental income for the land he owns, and an interest return on the capital he has invested. The obvious reason for this is that if he were not farming the land himself, he might spend his time earning a wage from some alternative employment (say in a factory or as an artisan); he might rent his land to some one else who would pay a rent for it; and he might invest his money in government bonds or other securities and receive interest on the investment. Whether the farm has been profitable in an economic sense can be determined only after a fair wage, rent, and interest have been deducted from the net income. A business can have a "net income" and still operate at a "loss."

Many small businesses operate year after year at a loss because they do not earn an income adequate to provide a normal wage or a reasonable rent and interest. Perhaps the entrepreneur has not thought of alternative ways he could use his time, land, and capital. More likely he has considered them but he places a personal value on the independence of being in business for himself. Or he may want to get out of business but fears a loss in the disposal of his property.

The bottom line of net income for a corporation is nearer to the profit that the corporation really makes than is true of the proprietorship or partnership. Before this income is calculated, all wages from the janitor to the president have been subtracted. But the remaining net income consists both of rent and interest on the one hand and a possible profit or loss on the other.

When all of these items are taken into consideration, actual profits are much smaller than most uninitiated people think. In fact, profits may be insignificant. Some economists who have studied these matters feel that in the long run profits and losses just about cancel out for all businesses as a whole. The number of entrepreneurs making good business judgments and earning substantial profits may be just about counterbalanced by the number of entrepreneurs who make poor business judgments and operate at a loss. When "business is good" the profits exceed the losses; when "business is bad" the losses exceed the profits. If the losses are severe the business may fail.

It is estimated that about 300,000 new businesses in the United States are formed each year and that approximately two-thirds of these will fail within the first five years of their life.[3] Naturally, many more fail in hard times than in good times but even in the best of times some will fail. The average life expectancy of a business is only about six years. One-third to one-half of all retail stores are discontinued within three years. This does not mean that all of these failures resulted in legal bankruptcy. But it certainly does mean that they were not making a profit and that the entrepreneur has decided to cut his losses by moving to some other line of business or moving out of business entirely. When one entrepreneur decides to leave a business someone else may enter the same or similar business. "The inalienable right to lose one's shirt is still highly cherished."

Much more could be said about the risks the entrepreneur assumes. His risks arise not only from the decisions he makes about the amount and kinds of labor, land, and capital he will use in the productive process. To an even greater extent the risks arise from decisions concerning the kind of product to be produced, the kinds of merchandise carried in inventory, or the kinds of services rendered. Is there an adequate demand for these things to enable him to charge a price sufficient to cover the costs? What quantities should be produced? What quality or style of produce should be manufactured? His past experience (or the experience of others in similar lines of business) may provide some guidelines, but since he must usually produce weeks or months before he can sell, he must forecast future demand. How successful he is in preparing these forecasts is another important factor in determining whether he will operate at a profit or a loss.

There are many more complicating factors, but I have

space to mention only one. Sometimes a business person's income statement year after year may show only very moderate income—so small as not to provide a reasonable wage for his labor, rent for his land, and interest for his capital. And then, after many such discouraging years, the business is sold for far more than the book value of its assets. This is not an unusual situation for the farmer. If the farmland was bought when prices of land were low, its value today may be ten, twenty, or in unusual cases, even many more times the price originally paid. These capital gains were not considered each year when income statements were prepared because they were not "realized." But if the farm is then sold when land prices are high, a very large profit results.

Here again the entrepreneur is a risk bearer. Land prices have gone up substantially in recent years, but they do not always advance. Sometimes they fall and there will be "capital losses." Even if the price of the land does not fall, the market price of the crops produced on the land may fall. The farmer is then left in the position of paying interest on money borrowed to buy the land and meet the taxes on the land out of a lower cash income than he had contemplated.

Profits and Capital Accumulation

The stock market is popularly thought to be the source of capital for business enterprise. Actually, it is primarily a means by which one stockholder's ownership shares can be readily transferred to another. No new capital is being accumulated in this process. Rather, new capital accumulation results from the sale of new issues of stocks or bonds or borrowing of money from banks or trade creditors. But even this kind of capital accumulation is small compared with the capital which results from plowing back into the business earnings and profits. Studies of the source of capital for business corporations show that in the past twenty years, approximately two-thirds of all capital accumulation stems from the reinvestment of past earnings. The sole proprietorship or the partnership is even more dependent on past earnings for the formation of new capital. Profits, therefore, are not only a reward for successful risk bearing. They also are an indispensable source of business growth and expansion.

This does not mean that profits and capital accumulation are the same. When the profits are reinvested in productive assets (e.g., plant, equipment, inventories) the owner does not receive an immediate *personal* benefit. However, it results in an immediate *social* benefit in the form of creating additional jobs or greater production of goods. On the other hand, if the one who receives the profits withdraws them from the business and spends them for consumer goods (personal or family use), there is an *individual* benefit but not a social benefit. The earning of a profit is not in itself either moral or immoral. It is neutral. The morality depends on the way the profits are used. Discussed further in chapter five.

The penalties for failure in risk bearing are, of course, not borne exclusively by the entrepreneur. If the enterprise fails, the entrepreneur may go into bankruptcy and thus shift part of the burden to the creditors. Business failure also means at least temporary unemployment for employees of the enterprise. The labor thus also bears a portion of the risk—how much depends on such factors as the worker's age, accumulated skills, and reemployability. In chapter two I will also show that in the past workers have often borne a substantial part of the real burden of capital accumulation.

Are Christian Entrepreneurs Different?

What I have been saying applies to all business persons,

whether they be Christian or not. But this book is about
Christian entrepreneurs. Are Christians better qualified than
non-Christians to enter business and to assume its risks?
Frederick B. Tolles of Swarthmore College wrote a book 30
years ago entitled *Meeting House and Counting House.*[4]
This book described changes in Quaker life and practice
during the first century following their migration from England to Pennsylvania. Tolles was particularly interested in
the growth of the Quaker merchant group in Philadelphia.
The earliest Quakers came from some of the poorest sections
of England. They came chiefly from the "lower strata of
English society."[5] More than three-fifths of them were
manual workers. But in less than a century after coming to
the New World, many of them had become wealthy. "Although ... Quakers probably constituted no more than one-
seventh of Philadelphia's population, they accounted for
more than half of those who paid taxes in excess of one
hundred pounds.... Of the wealthiest seventeen persons in
Philadelphia eight were Quakers in good standing and four
were men who had been reared in the faith.... Because
Quaker businessmen were known to be scrupulously honest
... customers flocked to do business with them."[6]

From the beginning the Quakers resembled the Mennonites in following the "ethic of love and nonresistance as
literally binding upon them as followers of Christ." But with
"this Anabaptist position ... they combined the essentially
Calvinistic conviction that religion must be integrated with
life on the natural plane."[7] The Quakers, therefore, did not
withdraw into relatively closed communities as the Mennonites tended to do but participated actively in political
and economic life. But the changes which came to the
Quakers in the eighteenth century have come to the Mennonites in the twentieth century. In spite of the many efforts

made to strengthen "Mennonite community" following World War II, rapid developments in transportation and communication inevitably meant that Mennonites became less isolated from the larger society. Rapid technological change in agricultural production meant that many fewer farmers were needed. Mennonites shifted away from primarily rural-farming occupations.

J. Howard Kauffman and Leland Harder, in their survey of Mennonites, found that in 1970 the proportion of Mennonites who were farm owners and managers was ten times that of the American population as a whole; the proportion of Mennonites in professional and technical occupations was twice that of other Americans; and the proportion of Mennonites who were business owners and managers was slightly higher than for other Americans. On the other hand, the proportion of Mennonites who were laborers, machine operators, and craftsmen was smaller than for other Americans.[8] It is probable that in the eight years which have passed since Kauffman and Harder made their survey, the proportion of Mennonites who are entrepreneurs has increased. But even if the 1970 figures still reflect the current situation, nearly 40 percent of Mennonite adults may be classified as entrepreneurs.

The number of Mennonites who engage in business is large and growing. Mennonites are no longer simply a "quiet country people." But the early Anabaptists weren't either. Claus-Peter Clasen's comprehensive list of "all known Anabaptists in South and Central Germany, Switzerland, and Austria" reveals that many of them had occupations such as "baker, hat-maker, city clerk, weaver, miller, cooper, tailor, cabinet maker, bottle maker, shoemaker, barber-surgeon, harness maker, schoolmaster, printer, professor, stone mason." Many of the artisans in this list doubtless also sold the products they made and therefore were small-scale entrepreneurs. Only a few were listed as "peasants" but many whose occupations were not recorded may also have been farmers.[9] Clearly many of them were engaged in business.

Menno Simons also recognized that many different occupational groups would exist side by side in the church: "judges, lawyers, preachers, merchants, and retailers." But he distinguished between "God-fearing merchants and retailers" and "wicked merchants and retailers." The distinguishing features were whether they were motivated by "this accursed thirst for profit," engaged in "false traffic and merchandise," or dealt "honestly." He urged that "they be circumspect in dealing and on the alert against moral danger."[10]

A Look Ahead

This book is written with the conviction that Christians will want to use the ethical insights of their faith in order to be more faithful Christian disciples in working as entrepreneurs. In chapter two I will examine biblical teachings concerning the productive process and will make some observations on how these biblical teachings can be applied to the problems of the modern world. Chapters three and four are an analysis of the ethical problems of the business person, again returning first to the biblical teachings, and from these teachings to some of the ethical dilemmas the entrepreneur faces in our day. In chapter five I will move from the ethical problems that arise within business to personal decisions concerning life-style, consumer patterns, and gifts to the church—not only because these decisions are important in their own right but also because they have important implications for the way a business is operated. In particular I will note how they influence capital formation. In chapter six I will analyze how entrepreneurs may use their financial resources in promoting the work of the church. Chapter seven is a discussion of forms of ownership other than privately-owned, free enterprise business—forms which some Christian entrepreneurs feel more closely meet the Christian ideal. Finally, chapter eight examines some ways in which the unique gifts of the entrepreneur may be utilized in the program of the church, both on the local congregational level and in churchwide boards and committees.

This book is written by one who has spent most of his life in educational administration and in teaching courses in economics and business. I believe deeply in and am committed to the work of the church in the local congregation, the conference, and churchwide boards and committees. But I have very little experience as an entrepreneur or businessman. Perhaps this should have disqualified me from writing this book.

Per Jacobsson was a Swedish economist who was for more than a quarter of a century economic adviser of the Bank for International Settlements in Basel. As a former managing director for the International Monetary Fund he "used to denounce the findings of theoretical economists of his time by saying that they always talk about money but never have any."[11] In spite of this well-placed warning, I have written this book to talk about money. I hope that it stimulates a continuing dialogue between those who have "made" money and those who only talk about it.

As a lifelong teacher of economics I have "talked" to many students about money. Teachers never know for sure whether they have "educated" their students or whether somehow their students have been able to secure a good education in spite of the teacher's mistakes. But many of my students (either because of or in spite of my teaching) have earned much more money than I have. This doesn't disturb me provided that they have earned their money in socially useful activity and that they have used the money they have earned in a Christian way. Similarly, it is incumbent on me to use the money I earn as a Christian teacher in a Christian way.

The problems I face as a Christian teacher are somewhat simpler than those the Christian business person faces as an entrepreneur. It is the purpose of this book to study some of these complexities. Because the topic of the book emphasizes that part of living which concerns material affairs, some of my readers may feel that I am more interested in material things than in spiritual things. But I firmly believe that Jesus taught that the attitudes we take toward the material world will strongly influence and determine our spiritual lives. How many business strategies, for instance, have been planned by business people while in church when their minds have wandered from the sermon? Lest you think that I am being anti-business in asking this question, let me hasten to add that a Christian teacher also faces the same temptation.

I have probably "personalized" or "individualized" the entrepreneurial function more than real-life experience permits. I have done this consciously because I have the opinion that most of my readers carry responsibilities in small businesses rather than in large corporations. Furthermore, I think there is a significant difference between the individual risk bearer and the institutionalized form of risk bearing in the large corporation. This difference stems from the much larger amounts of capital required for and the greater complexity of the operations of the large corporation. One of the most striking developments in large corporations in recent years is the formation of large conglomerates. Indeed, in the past decade more than 90 percent of the business combinations have been of the conglomerate type.

A single conglomerate corporation may engage in such widely diversified operations as building nuclear reactors, bottling soft drinks, and selling educational materials. One of the main purposes of conglomerate combinations is to reduce risk. When conglomerates carry on operations in several different countries, they are popularly called "multi-nationals." The ethics of the operation of businesses of this size and complexity is an interesting subject in itself but it is beyond the scope of this book. [12]

CHAPTER 2

The Productive Use of Wealth

The economist defines wealth as "useful material things which are owned by human beings." There are three parts of this definition and all three are important. To be wealth an item must be "useful." In chapter one I defined usefulness or utility as the capacity of a thing to satisfy a human want. I have books in my library which once represented wealth but which are now so out of date that they no longer satisfy any want which I or anyone else may have. Though such books are both material and are owned by a human being, they no longer represent wealth because they are no longer "useful."

Wealth refers to material things. Thereby it excludes what for the Christian is his most precious possession: his Christian faith. My faith is highly useful; it satisfies my most profound wants and needs. My faith is my own possession; therefore, it meets the criterion of being "owned" by a human being. But it is not wealth because it is not material.

I have no legal document certifying my ownership; my ownership of it is not registered at the county courthouse.

Wealth is owned by human beings. The air we breathe is highly useful; it satisfies such an important want that I could not live without it. Air is material. Although we cannot see it, we can feel it when it is in motion. Chemists can analyze it and inform us of the elements of which it is composed. But air is a free good; it is not owned by human beings. Therefore, it does not satisfy the third criterion in my definition and it cannot be considered wealth.

In chapter one I drew a distinction between land and capital—land being the God-given productive resources and capital the productive resources which have been produced by man. If one accepts the definition of wealth which I gave, both land and capital may be considered wealth since both are useful, material things owned by human beings. Both, of course, appear on the asset side of the balance sheet of a business enterprise. With proper husbanding, agricultural land can continue to be productive in perpetuity. Mineral resources are subject to depletion as they are mined, although some may be recycled; others, like petroleum, are lost once used. Capital, on the other hand, is subject to depreciation, obsolescence, or inadequacy. In other words, it wears out, becomes out of date, or is simply not large enough to be used efficiently any longer.

The Forms of Capital

Capital, too, may be divided into a number of subsidiary categories. We may distinguish between producers' capital, consumers' capital, social capital, and financial capital. Producers' capital consists of the buildings, machinery, and tools of the business enterprise. The entrepreneur expects it to produce a continuing stream of income from the time he

purchased it until he discards it or trades it in as fully de-
preciated. Consumers' capital is owned by consumers; they
too have purchased it with the expectation that it will
produce a series of returns. If the item will be worn out in
the course of weeks or months, we call it a nondurable
consumer capital item. Clothing is an obvious example of
this. If we expect that it will last for three or more years, we
call it a durable consumer good. Our furniture, automobile,
and home are such examples. Social capital consists of items
which we expect will produce a series of satisfactions over a
period of time but which are owned by a social group rather
than an individual. A hospital, school building, or public
highway are examples of social capital. Financial capital
consists of accounts receivable, business inventories, bank
accounts, or temporary investments. Usually the more
rapidly they are "turned over" the more productive they will
be for the entrepreneur.

Who Owns Wealth?

The definition of wealth does not specify who the human
beings are who assume the ownership of wealth. Under pure
communism all wealth is owned by "the people." Under
pure capitalism all wealth is privately owned by individuals.
In actual practice no society is purely communist or purely
capitalist. In the Soviet Union, for example, nondurable
consumer capital is all privately owned. Some durable
consumer goods are also privately owned. Most farm
families have effective ownership of the houses in which
they live. City dwellers are likely to live in publicly owned
apartment buildings, but even so it is estimated that 40
percent of all urban housing (located mainly in the smaller
towns and villages) is privately owned.

The goal of communist agriculture is the state farm or the

collective farm. A state farm is usually a very large farm owned by the government. Collective farms are somewhat smaller but they too are owned by the community rather than the individual. But on both of these types of farms there are likely to be private plots of from one-half to two acres which are owned by the farmer. A recent article in a Soviet journal reported that 27 percent of the total farm output comes from private plots that occupy less than one percent of the nation's agricultural lands.[1] In 1973, 62 percent of the potatoes, 32 percent of other vegetables and fruits, 47 percent of the eggs, and 34 percent of the meat and dairy products came from these private entrepreneurs in the Soviet Union. In some of the Eastern European communist countries, especially Poland and Yugoslavia, more than 80 percent of farmland is privately owned. .

But if communist countries are partially capitalistic so also capitalistic countries have large, publicly owned business enterprises. The importance of these governmentally owned and operated enterprises in all Western countries has been expanding constantly over the past several hundred years. In the United States at least 20 percent of all fixed capital formation is in the public, rather than the private, sector. In Canada this ratio is about 30 percent, and in many Western European countries it is 40 percent or more. In most of these countries the railroads, the airlines, telephone, telegraph, and radio and TV broadcasting, and often the production and sale of gas and electric power, are all in the hands of the government rather than private enterprise. The ethical problems of operating such governmental business obviously fall outside the scope of this book.

The Bible Speaks About Wealth

What does the Bible say about the productive use of

wealth? It is clear that the economic organization which existed in Bible times was much simpler than the complex society we know today. In fact, the German economic historian Werner Sombart[2] places the date for the beginning of capitalism at about AD 1000. The form of capitalism stemming from the Industrial Revolution is, of course, much more recent in origin. Most historians would say that the Industrial Revolution began about 1750. Modern finance capitalism is a still more recent development, starting about 100 years ago. Although the Bible was written long before the birth of any of these forms of capitalism, the Bible speaks concerning some economic practices which have developed through many years into modern capitalism. Various passages in the Bible indicate that in Bible times there were wage rates for labor, a rudimentary market system, an interest (usury) on loans, and wealth in the form of both land and capital.

The Bible makes it clear that the owner of all wealth is God and that God has entrusted these good things to man as his stewards. "The earth is the Lord's and the fulness thereof, the world and those who dwell therein" (Ps. 24:1). Land belongs to God. So does capital. The major form of capital in biblical times was cattle. "For every beast of the forest is mine, the cattle on a thousand hills" (Ps. 50:10). Whenever we speak of the "private sector" or of "private business enterprise" Christians must realize that we have adopted a secular vocabulary. For the Christian there is no real "private" ownership. God is the Owner.

Whether productive capital should be privately owned as in the United States and Canada or governmentally owned as in the Soviet Union is for the Christian a decision which must be made in the light of the prior fact that from the biblical standpoint neither the private entrepreneur nor the government *owns* the capital. The biblically significant question is what kind of stewardship can be devised which will enable us to be most faithful in carrying out God's will for his property.

I am of the opinion that for most things "private" ownership is superior to government ownership. I believe that this was also the situation in Bible times. But the biblical discussion of economic issues is filled with warnings against the spiritual dangers which stem from private ownership. One of the purposes of this book is to examine these warnings as they apply to our current practices. The Bible also suggests a "year of jubilee" as a check on long-term accumulations of wealth in the form of land. Another purpose of this book is to study ways in which "jubilee" living may be carried out by the Christian entrepreneur in today's complex economic order.

Productive Use of Land and Capital

Let us now look in a little more detail at some of the biblical teachings. The productive use of land is recognized in the Creation story itself. "And God said, 'Let the earth put forth vegetation, plants yielding seed, and fruit trees bearing fruit in which is their seed, each according to its kind, upon the earth.' And it was so. . . . And God saw that it was good" (Gen. 1:11-12). Similarly, the animals which constituted the major form of capital through much of ancient Hebrew history were created by God. "And God said, 'Let the earth bring forth living creatures according to their kinds: cattle and creeping things and beasts of the earth according to their kinds.' And it was so. . . . And God saw that it was good" (Gen. 1:24-25).

For many centuries the Hebrew people were nomadic herdsmen—often moving their animals relatively long

distances to find adequate grass and water. Under such circumstances the ownership of land was not as important as
the ownership of capital—their herds. In fact, one of the
wealthiest of these ancient peoples must have been Job. "He
had seven thousand sheep, three thousand camels, five
hundred yoke of oxen, and five hundred she-asses, and very
many servants; so that this man was the greatest of all the
people of the east" (Job 1:3). No mention is made of the
number of acres of land that he owned. When his fortunes
were restored after his trials at the hand of Satan his capital
was doubled, but again no mention is made of his land (Job
42:12).

Animals were the most important form of capital
recognized in the Bible but other forms were present as well.
Vineyards were an important form of producers' capital
(e.g., Neh. 5:3). Olive trees were planted and olive presses
established to provide oil. The garden across the Kidron in
Jerusalem where Jesus went with his disciples on the night of
his betrayal was called "Gethsemane"—a word which
means "oil press" (Jn. 18:1; Mt. 26:36). There was capital in
the form of farm tools such as the ax (2 Kings 6:5), the goads,
the plowshares, and the mattocks (1 Sam. 13:21). In a New
Testament parable Jesus spoke of a rich farmer who found
his barns inadequate and had to build "larger ones" to
"store all my grain and my goods" (Lk. 12:18). These barns
were also capital. Hammers and tools of iron were needed
for the building trades (1 Kings 6:7). The flourishing foreign
trade carried on by King Solomon required that he build a
"fleet of ships at Ezion-geber, which is near Eloth on the
shore of the Red Sea" (1 Kings 9:26). These ships carried
gold and silver as well as chariots and horses (1 Kings 10:29).

The ancient Hebrews knew how to refine metal ores (Is.
1:25). This would have required capital equipment, but

"Solomon's mines" were probably for copper or iron rather than gold and silver. Glueck's explorations in South Palestine indicate that there was a very extensive copper and iron mining industry between the Dead Sea and the Gulf of Aqabah.[3] Moses promised the children of Israel that in Canaan they would find "a land whose stones are iron, and out of whose hills you can dig copper" (Deut. 8:9). The author of Job was acquainted with silver, gold, iron, and copper mines and referred to the "deep darkness" in the "shafts" where mining operations and the "smelting" of the refining process took place (Job 28:1-4). David may already have exploited the salt mines of Edom (2 Sam. 8:13-14).

Not only was there producers' capital in Bible times; there was financial capital as well. The gold and silver already referred to comes under this category, though it may have been partly used for decorative purposes and thus was a form of consumers' capital. They had accounts receivable (Lk. 16:5-7), inventories (Mt. 13:30), and mortgages (Neh. 5:3). There was social capital. The temple of Solomon and its furnishings constituted a very substantial investment in social capital (1 Kings 7:2-51). Another, though probably much less costly, form of social capital were the weapons and armor of war (1 Sam. 17:38). Samuel warned his people that under a kingship these items would become more costly and would constitute a real drain on the economic resources of their society (1 Sam. 8:11 ff.). Finally, there was consumers' capital in the form of tents, clothing, bowls (Amos 6:6), and some very costly houses for the wealthy with "beds of ivory" (Amos 6:4).

Land and the Year of Jubilee

In the early history of Israel and through the period of the Patriarchs the Hebrews were a nomadic people. But when they entered the land of Canaan following their sojourn out of Egypt, the land was allocated to the various tribes (Josh. 13 to 19). When the Levitical code was established it was recognized that unrestricted land ownership was a danger and that limitations should be placed on the private ownership of land. Inevitably some people would be more successful in their use of the land than others and over the course of time inequalities would develop which would threaten the stability of Hebrew society.

Hebrews were reminded that "land shall not be sold in perpetuity, for the land is mine; for you are strangers and sojourners with me" (Lev. 25:23). But if they had to sell some of their land and did not have the money to buy it back, the land would be returned to them ("released") on the year of jubilee. This year of jubilee was the "fiftieth year" when a "loud trumpet" was sent "abroad . . . throughout all your land" (Lev. 25:9). Similarly, if any one of the children of Israel was sold into slavery to another Israelite to satisfy a debt, he should not be considered "as a slave: he shall be with you as a hired servant and as a sojourner. He shall serve with you until the year of the jubilee" and then he shall be released to return to his own land (Lev. 25:34-41).

It is not clear whether the Levitical rules for the year of jubilee were actually carried out in practice. In fact it is probable that the rules were bypassed or ignored. We know that Isaiah found it necessary to prophesy against "those who join house to house, who add field to field, until there is no more room, and you are made to dwell alone in the midst of the land" (Is. 5:8). The year of jubilee was intended to prevent just this kind of excess accumulation of land. Although the Levitical rules do not mention a redistribution of cattle (a major form of capital in Bible times), this was probably implied by the redistribution of land. Since lands were necessary to support herds, the jubilean redistribution of land would have entailed a restriction in the size of the accumulation of cattle as well. And Jeremiah prophesied against those who were not keeping the sabbatical rules for the freedom of Hebrew slaves (Jer. 34:8-17).

In his sermon at the synagogue in Nazareth, Jesus said that Isaiah's prophecy of "the acceptable year of the Lord" has "today . . . been fulfilled in your hearing" (Lk. 4:19, 21). John H. Yoder has suggested that his hearers interpreted this correctly as meaning that the year of jubilee is now a reality under the messianic kingdom Jesus was establishing.[4]

Present-Day Implications of Biblical Concepts of Wealth

What are some of the implications of the biblical concepts of the productive use of wealth for the Christian entrepreneur in the twentieth century? I would like to suggest three.

In the first place, the biblical teachings have always been supremely relevant in every age, but developments within our own lifetime have given these teachings an even more urgent importance. The reasons for the present urgency are two: first, the world has a vastly greater population today than existed in Bible times or in any other period of past history; and second, the need for the extensive use of capital in the productive process is greater than it has been at any time previously.

World Population: Enormous Expansion Since Bible Times

No one knows precisely what the world's population was in Bible times. Estimates have recently been made by the United Nations but they are obviously very rough because no regular census was taken and the ones taken covered very small areas of the earth. In fact, there were strong taboos against the numbering of people (2 Sam. 24). But the estimate by United Nations demographers of the world's population at the time of Christ—about 130 million people—gives at least a rough approximation.

An even more important fact than the absolute numbers is the hypothesis that the world's population was in those days increasing very slowly—doubling perhaps every 1,000 years. By the time the first colonies were established in North America early in the seventeenth century, the world population had grown to about 500 million people; in other words, world population was now doubling in about 800 years. Though the rate of population growth had increased slightly, the growth was still very slow indeed. To use terms that the population experts use: the birth rate was just about matched by the death rate; as a result the rate of natural increase was very small.

Beginning about 1730 the rate of population growth started to increase dramatically. Instead of doubling every 1,000 years as it had in ancient times, or every 800 years in early modern times, it doubled in approximately 175 years between 1650 and 1825. Then from 1825 until 1935 the world population doubled again—this time in a period of only 90 years. At present rates of population growth the population is now doubling about every 30 to 35 years. Each day the world's population is increasing by about 270,000 persons. This means that now in only a little over one year the number of *additional* mouths to feed and bodies to be clothed is equal to the *total* who had to be provided for at the time of Christ. With an estimated current world population of four billion persons, there are thirty-one people today for each person who lived at the time of Christ.

Both birth rates and death rates have been falling in recent years, but the death rate has been falling much more rapidly than the birth rate. This is true both in highly developed societies and in lesser developed areas. I need not belabor the reasons for the decline in the death rate in recent decades. Medical science has advanced enormously with the discovery of medicines to cure infectious diseases. Vaccination and innoculation have virtually eliminated some diseases which were once the scourge of millions. Better nutrition and sanitary facilities have also contributed mightily. The problem of feeding, clothing, and providing other essential services for this enormous and rapidly increasing number of people is both a production and a distribution problem. In chapter one I defined production as the creation of place, time, and ownership utility (distribution and marketing) as well as form utility (manufacturing, construction, and agriculture). The needs of the world's more than four billion people cannot be met unless *all* available productive resources are carefully husbanded and used.

This production problem was first recognized about 1800 by a young English clergyman, Thomas Robert Malthus, who argued with his father each day at breakfast time on the perfectibility of the human race. Young Malthus became so agitated that he published his views of the problem in 1798 in a small book *Essay on the Principle of Population*. In this book he argued that, unless checked by the food supply, there was a tendency for population to double every twenty-five years. Any one who has worked with figures of geometric progression can easily see what these figures would mean: 1, 2, 4, 8, 16, 32, 64, 128, 256, 512, 1,024, 2,048 ... and so on. Before many years even our vast world would not have standing room. But Malthus thought that the means of subsistence would tend to increase by an arithmetic ratio: 1, 2, 3, 4, 5, 6, 7, 8.... Already in eight generations the population would be 16 times the means of subsistence and in twelve generations the population would be 171 times the means of subsistence. Of course the disparity between the two would continue to accelerate.

Malthus did not say that population would actually increase as rapidly as his figures of geometric progression would suggest. He only said that there would be a *tendency* in this direction. He thought that there would be *positive* checks on the death rate—war, famine, and pestilence. But the outlook was so pessimistic that the English essayist Thomas Carlyle dubbed economics "the dismal science"—an epithet which has stuck even though the pessimistic forecasts have not been realized. In later editions of his *Essay*, Malthus took a less pessimistic view by suggesting that *preventive* checks might serve to reduce the birth rate. He was not thinking of what we normally call birth control today (which has undoubtedly been a powerful force in reducing the birth rate in developed countries more substantially than Malthus had expected). Rather he meant "moral restraint," the postponement of marriage until a family could be supported.

Malthus' preventive checks have been operating, probably more effectively than he thought possible. But the avoidance of the early doom which Malthus envisaged has not been the result of the decline in the birth rate as much as the increase in the production of the means of subsistence. The industrial, agrarian, and commercial revolutions mentioned in chapter one had just got underway when Malthus wrote. Tremendously productive agricultural lands were opened for cultivation in the Western Hemisphere and in Oceania. The mechanization of agricultural production enabled more crops to be produced with fewer workers. Improvements in transportation (especially the steamship across the Atlantic) made this food available for the growing population of Europe. The development of hybrid seeds, fertilizers, and pesticides substantially improved crop yields. Total farm output expanded even though more and more land is devoted to shopping centers, parking lots, suburban sprawl, and the great highway systems with their cloverleafs. (Someone has said that the cloverleaf should be the U.S. national flower!)

Capital: Essential for Today's Production

The doomsday forecast by Malthus has been negated by an unprecedented application of capital to the productive process. This capital has not only taken the form of sophisticated agricultural machinery and the industrial base needed to manufacture it; it also includes the social capital represented in educational institutions, agricultural experiment stations, and extension services which have enabled us to realize substantial technological improvements in production. Many ethical issues stem from this increasing use of capital and the social problems which have resulted from it. Some of these will be considered elsewhere in this book. But the important thing to note here is that we must face these problems squarely; we cannot meet them by a simplistic return to a pre-capitalistic economic order. Individuals can doubtless gain a certain nostalgic satisfaction by simple subsistence organic farming. But this is not an option for a world in which there are already four billion mouths to feed and where thirty-five years from now there will probably be twice that many. Whether we like it or not, we have to use all of the factors of production, including a liberal and growing use of capital. The Christian participant in this process will have to come to grips with the ethical dilemmas which it raises.

The extensive use of capital in the productive process has

made the economies of the "developed" world (North America, Western Europe and Japan) highly prosperous. This fact has not been lost among thinkers in other parts of the world. In the Third World (the less developed countries or LDCs) there is an acute shortage of all kinds of capital: factories, utilities, transportation equipment, homes, schools, roads, and hospitals. But for an LDC the accumulation of capital, especially in the early stages, may be a slow and painful process. As noted in chapter one, all capital is the result of saving. But when the vast majority of the population is living at the subsistence level, as in the LDCs, saving is extremely costly in terms of human effort and sacrifice.

The return on some kinds of capital investments, for example a manufacturing plant, is realized rather soon after the investment is made. But the return on other highly necessary capital investments in LDCs, though large in the long run, is often delayed by ten or more years. An important example of this is investment in elementary education. School buildings must be built, teachers' salaries must be paid, books and supplies must be purchased. In addition to these easily recognizable costs of investment in educational capital, we sometimes forget the costs involved in the fact that, while the children are being educated, they have been removed from other productive services they may have been rendering their families. It is urgent that the developed countries of the world recognize these problems and that we do what can be done to reduce the burden which people in the LDCs have been experiencing. I will be making some concrete suggestions on this in chapter six.

Capital Accumulation: Cause for Suffering

It is hard to overestimate the suffering which capital accumulation causes in the early stages. Although some of the burden of this accumulation rests on the entrepreneur, the most onerous burden is diffused far more widely throughout the economy. Historically, in the West much of the burden has taken the form of low wages, long hours, and even human servitude. It was a system of slave labor which built the somewhat shaky economy of the American antebellum South. But the extensive use of child labor in late eighteenth- and early nineteenth-century England was scarcely less reprehensible.

The sweat-shop conditions in manufacturing enterprises in the American North may also have been just about as costly in human terms as the outright slavery of the South. As late as 1900 the working day in the American steel industry was often 12 hours, the working week 84 hours. As the workers sacrificed in this way, capital was being accumulated. This capital in turn made later generations of workers vastly more productive and enabled the entrepreneurs employing the workers to pay much higher wage rates. But this future promise was not a present reality to workers who faced the dreary factory conditions of less than a century ago.

The developed countries of the world are already highly capitalistic in their methods of production. The poor of the LDCs aspire to becoming more capitalistic but they are not sure what economic course of action would be most rewarding. But there is another large segment of the world's people living in what we call communist or socialist economies. Nearly half the world's people now live under communism. First, the USSR some 60 years ago, and now all of Eastern Europe, the vast population of China, Cuba, North Korea, Vietnam and other parts of Southeast Asia, and some parts of Africa now embrace communism.

However, in practice the communist countries seek to be-

come the most "capitalistic" of all. Through centrally devised and administered plans they seek to force rapid accumulation of capital. The productive powers of their
economies are directed toward production and accumulation
of capital goods. This has been achieved in part by a de-em-
phasis on consumer goods. The workers in these countries
work long hours at low rates of pay. People in the Soviet
Union suffered in the 1930s at least as much as the people in
Great Britain during the 1840s when Friedrich Engles
criticized Britain so severely for exploitation. Consumer
goods in the communist countries are in chronically short
supply and are often of poor quality. The international trade
of communist countries is hampered because when they do
have consumer goods available for export they find it difficult to sell them in competition with higher quality goods
which are already available in Western markets.

On the other hand, there is an enormous demand in communist countries for the consumer goods of capitalist countries. Special stores (called Pewex) handling such goods have
been established in a number of cities in Poland but only
customers having dollars or other "hard" currencies can
make purchases. Similar stores have been established in the
Soviet Union.

A dispatch from the Associated Press quoted *Pravda* (the
official Soviet communist newspaper) as criticizing the
quality of consumer goods. The report quoted a decree from
the Communist Party Central Committee and the Council
of Ministers. It "reflected high-level dissatisfaction with Soviet retail trade which ... irks shoppers with shortages,
crowded stores, long lines, surly service, and waiting lists for
scarce items. Residents of some cities near Moscow
frequently undertake all-day bus rides to the capital to obtain eggs, canned milk, and fruit because they are unavail-

able locally."[5] Formal rationing of sewing machines, bicycles, watches, transistor radios, and other items "not absolutely needed" is maintained in China.[6] All of this, of course, means that communist countries place a very high priority on capital accumulation and have squeezed the consumer to make it possible.

The farmer in the Soviet Union has also suffered in this effort to accumulate capital rapidly. In classical Marxist theory the leadership for the communist revolution should come from the urban "proletariat," the urban workers. But in outlining this theory Karl Marx had in mind Great Britain and other industrialized Western countries. But the first communist revolution came instead to Russia which was relatively backward economically; Russia was still such a predominantly agrarian society that the industrial proletariat was too small to carry the burden of leadership. Instead, the much more numerous agricultural laborers had to do so. They contributed to capital accumulation by centrally determined and controlled farm procurement prices. These prices were so low as to keep the farmer in poverty. Periodic rural uprisings in protest against the system were ruthlessly suppressed.

Capitalistic countries of the industrial West attained their high levels of economic growth and their present high levels of consumption of consumer goods through the accumulation and use of capital in the productive process. LDCs today are also trying to accumulate capital as a means of lifting themselves out of their poverty. Communist countries have used ruthless devices for rapid capital accumulation. The Christian entrepreneur of our day cannot compete successfully unless he also makes an extensive use of capital. The first question (what is the Christian attitude toward the accumulation and use of capital?) has a simple answer. He must accumulate it and he must use it.

But this answer is too simple. Capital is amoral. Like power, it is either good or bad depending on the purposes for which it is used. Furthermore, it may be accumulated in immoral ways. Slavery was an example of this in past generations. Methods which defraud the government or oppress the worker or the consumer are examples today.

Who Should "Own" Capital?

The second question is: who should "own" and "control" the use of capital? The psalmist said that "the cattle on a thousand hills" are God's. Since cattle constituted the main form of wealth in biblical times, it would seem to be a fair interpretation of the biblical viewpoint to hold that in the modern highly capitalistic economies the real owner of capital is not the government (as in the Soviet Union), nor the stockholders of great corporations (as in the United States), nor the tiny capital of the shoe shine boys on the streets of Nairobi (as in many LDCs). The real and ultimate owner is *God*.

It is easy to pay lip service to this concept in a Sunday school class. It is much more difficult to give it meaning in actual business practice. A businessman who has accumulated capital because he and his family have deliberately limited their consumption of consumer goods while his neighbor (often a fellow member of his church) has spent all that he has earned on consumer goods is likely to have a gut feeling that the capital he has accumulated is *his*. We joke: "It is wonderful what you and God have done to this farm." "Yes, but you should have seen it when God had it all to himself." But at the same time the joke may well reflect our real feelings.

We need not belittle our personal efforts in capital accumulation nor any genuine self-denial which has accompanied it; yet it is well to remind ourselves that capital accumulation is a complex process. It has extended over years—perhaps generations. We make use today of a technology which has been built up over many years by the laborious work of many people. These technological improvements enable us today to be more productive than was true in previous ages. Since we are more productive today we can save more from our current income and make less onerous sacrifices in the process. An earlier generation made the real sacrifices. Sometimes in our production today we benefit from inherited wealth—from parents and grandparents who sacrificed to give us a good education, good health care, good nutrition, and perhaps that crucial nest egg of financial capital which gave us a head start in comparison with our business competitors.

We hire workers who have been educated at public expense; we use highways and airports which have been built with tax dollars; we use farm methods which have been tested at government expense in governmentally operated agricultural universities and experiment stations. It is not just a matter of Christian humility to confess that all of our property really belongs to God; it is an economic fact that much of our capital has been accumulated by social processes which have been going on over a long period of time. They started long before our own lifetime of work.

Who Should Defend Capital Ownership?

In the third place, the Christian should recognize that responsible stewardship of all wealth (including capital) is not only a Christian duty; failure to exercise this kind of stewardship may result in gradual erosion of our wealth through government policies or in radical revolution. The

Old Testament prophets often made a list of faulty economic attitudes of the children of Israel (e.g., Is. 5 ff.) and then exclaimed "Ah, Assyria, the rod of my anger, the staff of my fury! Against a godless nation I send him ... to take spoil and seize plunder" (Is. 10:5, 6). They thought they had an adequate system of defensive alliances to prevent this. Isaiah said they won't work: "You are relying on Egypt, that broken reed of a staff, which will pierce the hand of any man who leans on it. Such is Pharaoh king of Egypt to all who rely on him" (Is. 36:6).

The twentieth-century counterpart of this ancient attitude is reliance upon military defense to protect "the American way of life." If we really thought that our property belonged to God we would be willing to trust God in its defense. But if in actuality we regard the property as our own, there is a subtle temptation to place its defense in our own hands.

Land Reform

Land reform is an urgent necessity in many parts of the world. I already commented on the jubilee principle of ancient Israel in which land was to be evenly distributed among the people who farmed it and then redistributed every fifty years to correct inequities which had developed in the previous half century. In sharp contrast the ownership of land in some LDCs today is concentrated in the hands of a few very wealthy, often absentee, landlords; the people who till the soil are miserably poor tenants. This was the situation in China under the Kuomintang of Chiang Kai-shek. Indeed, the communists there were often referred to in those days as "agrarian reformers." It was the situation in Ethiopia before the recent revolution which removed Emperor Haile Selassie from the throne and dispossessed the landlords (the Orthodox Church and the Imperial family).

One of the reasons for the remarkable growth of the economy of Japan in the post-World War II period was the land reform which was an integral part of the occupation policy of General MacArthur. People who owned land but were not farming it were forced to sell it in small parcels at pre-war, and therefore ridiculously low, prices to the people who were actually farming it. The result was a sharp decrease in political radicalism on the one hand and an enormous increase in agricultural productivity on the other.

The agrarian revolution in the United States and Canada in recent years has resulted in a marked increase in the average size of farms. Most of these farms are still farmed by individual entrepreneurs. But in some cases farming has become the activity of large farm corporations. Some observers think that in the next decade or two further movement in this direction will be accelerated. Quite apart from the economics of the matter, I have grave reservations whether such a concentration of land ownership will maintain the biblical principles of the divine ownership of wealth.

CHAPTER 3

Christian Ethics in Business: General Principles

In this chapter and in chapter four I will consider the ethical problems facing the Christian entrepreneur. I will look first at some of the explicit biblical teachings on this subject. Second, I will examine some teachings which are implicit—most of which arise from an extension of biblical concepts to business practices which have developed since Bible times. Finally, and this will be the largest part of these chapters, I want to survey some of the ethical dilemmas facing Christian entrepreneurs today.

The Bible and Business: Demands for High Ethical Principles
Some explicit biblical teachings on business are not only biblical: they are widely considered as "good business" as well. Raymond Baumhart, former dean of the School of Business Administration of Loyola University, has made the most detailed study of the attitudes toward ethics in business as held by American business people. He interviewed 100

businessmen and he sent a detailed questionnaire to a carefully selected list of 1,600 subscribers to the *Harvard Business Review*. He concluded that ethical considerations are important to American businessmen. "Perhaps the best criterion for judging how important ethics is to a person is how much he sacrifices—in terms of position, money, time, and energy—in order to act ethically." He reported that 83 percent of the persons he interviewed "provided examples of decisions they made for ethical reasons despite personal disadvantage.... However, a sizable minority ... displayed insensitivity to ethical issues ... How important is ethics to businessmen? Probably no more important than it is to the average American."[1]

Baumhart found that there was no significant difference in the ethical responses of business people who were affiliated with a church or synagogue and those who were not.[2] However, David Burks, chairman of the division of business of Harding College, attempted to learn whether business people who are financial supporters of conservative Harding College are more ethical than the general average of those included in the Baumhart sample. He sent the same questionnaire to 100 members of the Harding College Development Council which Baumhart had used for a cross section of subscribers to *Harvard Business Review*. He concluded that his select group of Christian businessmen "consistently indicated a stronger and more positive sense of ethical values." Furthermore, "Most Christian businessmen consider themselves more ethical than the average businessmen."[3]

Weights and Measures

The Bible is explicit in stating that weights and measures shall be accurate and just. "You shall do no wrong in judgment, in measures of length or weight or quantity. You shall have just balances, just weights.... I am the Lord your God" (Lev. 19:35, 36). "You shall not have in your bag two kinds of weights, a large and a small. You shall not have in your house two kinds of measures, a large and a small. A full and just weight you shall have, a full and just measure you shall have" (Deut. 25:13-15). Proverbs declared that "A false balance is an abomination to the Lord, but a just weight is his delight" (Prov. 11:1; see also 20:23). The prophets also gave stern warnings against false weights or balances. Micah asked, "Shall I acquit the man with wicked scales and with a bag of deceitful weights?" (Mic. 6:11; see also Hos. 12:7; Amos 8:5; Ezek. 45:10). In the Sermon on the Plain Jesus referred to a "good measure, pressed down, shaken together" (Lk. 6:38). Although the context would suggest that Jesus was referring primarily to spiritual matters, at least he was using accepted ethical business principles to illustrate spiritual truth.

Weights and measures used in business today are carefully prescribed by the Bureau of Standards and are tested periodically by government inspectors. The overt cheater is not only in danger of fine or imprisonment; he is engaging in bad business practices. But the temptation still remains and entrepreneurs sometimes yield to it. Perhaps the correct weight is given in fine print on the box but a larger than necessary box is used to give a false impression of the quantity of the contents. Or the term applied "large" may obscure the fact that it is really a middle-sized portion and that there are also "extra large" and "jumbo" sizes available!

The seller of a product may describe only its merits and deliberately conceal its faults. The rust spots on a used car may have been repaired and repainted so that it "looks nice" but will soon deteriorate again. A house may appear to be well insulated and yet be very expensive to heat adequately in cold weather. Suburban land may be sold for development purposes even though the seller knows that effective development is neither likely nor feasible. Insurance policies may contain many paragraphs of fine print which are a burden for the buyer to read but which outline exclusions or exemptions that materially reduce the value of the insurance offered. *Caveat emptor* is the Latin phrase which means "let the buyer beware." The doctrine means that the buyer is subject to all risks of a transaction except what constitutes outright fraud and certain implied warranties. Legally, a seller may follow this doctrine; the Christian entrepreneur lives by biblical principles which stand in judgment of it.

The Bible demands honesty not only with respect to weights and measures but in all interpersonal relationships. Bearing a false witness was condemned in the Ten Commandments (Ex. 20:16). Paul admonished the Ephesians to speak "the truth in love" (Eph. 4:15). But modern business is not always characterized by truth. A student was reported to have received the highest grade in his "Competitive Decision Making course at Harvard Business School because 'I was willing to lie to get a better score.' " Students find that hiding certain facts, bluffing, or even outright lying often gets them a better deal. But the professor in charge of the course insisted that his goals in the course were not "to teach them to lie" but rather "to teach them they may be lied to."[4] What a contrast to the tradition of Christian people whose "word is as good as their bond" and who seek to follow complete integrity in business as well as all other human relations.

Paying Workers a Just Wage

The Bible teaches the prompt payment of a just wage.

"You shall not oppress a hired servant . . . whether he is one of your brethren or one of the sojourners who are in your land within your towns; you shall give him his hire on the day he earns it, before the sun goes down" (Deut. 24:14, 15; see also Lev. 19:13).

Although modern business is highly capitalistic, labor costs often constitute by far the largest single element in business expenses. One of the most troublesome ethical problems faced by the Christian entrepreneur is the appropriate wage level to maintain in his business. This problem will be examined in detail shortly; at this point it must be observed that throughout history businessmen have tended to hold down wage levels in order to accumulate capital. A system of slavery has the economic effect of holding labor costs to the actual level of human subsistence. It is an utter denial of the value of human personality because it makes a human being in essence a piece of capital, like cattle, which can be bought and sold. Family units were often ruthlessly destroyed in the process; human dignity was utterly negated.

In practice, however, a "free labor" system also has its inhuman elements. Since a slave was valuable property, his owner had an economic incentive to provide adequate food, clothing, medical care, and shelter to keep the slave alive and well. The death of a slave was an economic loss. But in the initial stages of the Industrial Revolution the migration of workers from rural to urban areas provided entrepreneurs with what appeared to be a virtually inexhaustible supply of labor. If one worker died because his pay was not adequate for his subsistence, there were always other workers available to take his place.

Economic theories were thought to justify low wages for workers. In fact, there was no alternative but that wages be kept to the bare level of subsistence. David Ricardo, famous

British economist of the early nineteenth century, argued that there is a "natural price" of labor. This "is that price which is necessary to enable the labourers, one with another, to subsist and to perpetuate their race, without either increase or diminution."[5] The market price of labor might go above the "natural price" for only a short time, because economic forces would soon drive the price back to the "natural" level of subsistence. If "the market price of labor exceeds its natural price," such high wages would stimulate an increase in the population, according to the population theories of Malthus. With such an increase in the supply of laborers "wages again fall to their natural price, and indeed from a reaction sometimes fall below it." In this case the labor supply is reduced somewhat by the increased number of deaths caused by the lack of sufficient subsistence. Population would adjust so that "the supply of labourers will always ultimately be in proportion to the means of supporting them."[6] Ricardo's "iron law of wages," as it was frequently called, was a comfort for the rich because it seemed to justify the low rates of wages which they paid their employees, as well as to give this practice the status of a natural law comparable to the laws of physics.

Child labor was the scourge of the early factory system. Much of the new machinery in the factories was operated by children at very low wages. In fact, oftentimes children were simply "apprenticed" at no wage at all. The Elizabethan Poor Law of 1601 had directed that destitute children and orphans should be apprenticed to some trade. The factories abused this privilege and the parents felt forced to cooperate. The wages of parents were so low that they did not have the income needed to feed and clothe their children. So they legally "apprenticed" them to factories at the age of 7 or younger, where they worked with no pay other than their keep until the age of 21. But the children were crowded in the factories, they were badly overworked, an illness known as "putrid fever" often broke out, and the death rate of the children has been estimated at from 60 to 70 percent.[7]

The British *First Report on Mines 1842* reported children of 12 to 16 years (but sometimes as young as 8) working in mines as "pushers." The conditions they worked in were described this way: "A girdle is put around the naked waist, to which a chain from the carriage is hooked and passed between the legs, and the boys crawl on their hands and knees, drawing the carriage after them.... A sub-commissioner met a boy crying and bleeding from a wound in the cheek, and his master explained that the child was one of the slow ones who would move only when he saw blood, and that by throwing a piece of coal at him for that purpose he had accomplished his object."[8] Complete slavery was scarcely less depraved than this. At least child labor was an utter mockery of biblical teachings on the prompt payment of a just wage.

The "horror stories" taken from British history of a century and a half ago seem removed from the problems of the Christian entrepreneur today. The issues now deal with the demands of labor unions, competitive wage levels, the bases for wage differentials, job security, and fringe benefits. These topics are the subject of chapter four.

Biblical Teaching on Payment of Interest

The Bible also teaches against the payment (or receipt) of interest. "You shall not lend upon interest to your brother, interest on money, interest on victuals, interest on anything that is lent for interest. To a foreigner you may lend upon interest" (Deut. 23:19, 20; see also Ex. 22:25 and Lev. 25:36-

37). This was also a common practice among other ancient peoples. For example, in Babylon interest on produce was expressed as one third of the loan (rather than the equivalent of 33 1/3 percent) and the interest on money at one fifth (20 percent); from some ancient tablets interest rates as high as 50 percent were not unknown. Exorbitant rates of interest were viewed as a social plague and were vehemently condemned by the prophets (Ezek. 18:8; see also Neh. 5:6-13). Proverbs viewed interest income as essentially unstable and unprofitable in the long run (Prov. 28:8). Jesus reaffirmed the teachings against interest in his injunction to "lend, expecting nothing in return" (Lk. 6:35).

The medieval church attempted to follow these biblical teachings and to support them by referring to Aristotle who taught that money was barren (useful only as a medium of exchange). Thomas Aquinas urged an absolute prohibition of usury. Papal legislation on this subject began in 1175 but at first only spiritual penalties were imposed. However, Pope Gregory X at the Council of Lyons (1274) decreed that usurers should be prohibited from renting houses or even dwelling on lands. To enforce this regulation the Council stipulated that the wills of the unrepentant should be considered to be without effect. Pope Clement V at the Council of Vienna (1312) declared all secular legislation in favor of usury null and void.[9] "Florence was the financial capital of medieval Europe; but even at Florence the secular authorities fined bankers right and left for usury in the middle of the fourteenth century, and, fifty years later, first prohibited credit transactions altogether, and then imported Jews to conduct a business forbidden to Christians."[10]

The Protestant Reformation made no immediate changes. In fact, "For the arts by which men amass wealth and power, as for the anxious provision which accumulates for the future, Luther had all the distrust of a peasant and a monk." Luther's sermons or tracts on usury follow "doctrines . . . drawn from the straightest interpretation of ecclesiastical jurisprudence, unsoftened by qualifications" which by Luther's time some Catholic theologians were making.[11] And so, "It was predominantly Catholic cities which were the commerce capitals of Europe, and Catholic bankers who were its leading financiers."[12] Menno Simons also was stern in his warning against usury. He associated it with the sin of avarice and stated forthrightly that usurers were in need of conversion.[13]

Today we usually assume that the biblical teachings against interest apply to usury, and we define usury as an unjustifiably high rate of interest. Most biblical passages referring to "interest" in the Revised Standard Version were translated as "usury" in the King James Version but it is improbable that the word was used in the pejorative sense we think of it today. And so we have to reckon with the fact that the Bible actually condemned interest and that the medieval Catholic Church and early Protestant churches tried to apply these teachings literally. But as the economic order became more capitalistic, teachings against interest were no longer followed, first in Catholic areas and later in Protestant areas.

It is interesting to observe that in the twentieth century Islam is trying to maintain a prohibition of interest similar to that of medieval Catholicism and early Protestantism. Prince Mohammed Al-Faisal, son of the late King Faisal of Saudi Arabia, in an interview with the managing editor of popular economics journal *Challenge*,[14] reported that he is interested in developing a system of interest-free banking for Saudi Arabia. Islamic rules on interest stem from Islam's dependence on Old Testament principles. Saudi Arabian banks now operate on a profit-sharing basis with industries receiving loans. If the industry makes a profit, a portion of this is shared with the bank; we would call it interest on the loan. If the industry receiving the loan does not make a profit it is obligated to return the principal only.

Usury regulations were possible within the Hebrew or Christian community when most loans were made for consumptive purposes to help an unfortunate brother. But when it was recognized that capital is actually a factor of production, and when loans were made for productive uses in business purposes, the payment of interest did not seem inappropriate. In fact, all through the Middle Ages churches accepted and lived on rent from land. Though called a rent, an element of interest was also doubtless present in this income from land.[15]

It is dangerous to assume that Jesus was approving of the statements and actions of all the characters in his parables. In the parable of the talents, for instance, the master criticized the lassitude of the one-talented person by saying, "You ought to have invested my money with the bankers, and at my coming I should have received what was my own with interest" (Mt. 25:27). This should not be interpreted as Jesus' approval of interest.[16] In another of Jesus' parables the rich man commended a "dishonest steward for his prudence" (Lk. 16:1-8), but we should not conclude from this that Jesus meant to teach that his disciples engage in this type of selfish and shrewd business practice. Nor does Jesus' commendation of the faith of the centurion at Capernaum (Mt. 8:5-13) imply that Jesus sought to indoctrinate his followers on the efficacy of a military career as a way to eternal life.

It seems fair to conclude that the modern application of biblical teachings would include interest-free loans within the family and the church when these loans have been made for consumption purposes in response to recognized needs. At the same time loans made to provide capital for production may bear an interest provided the rate does not take undue advantage of the borrower.

Biblical Teaching on Litigation

The Bible also teaches against the use of litigation. Jesus taught "If any one would sue you and take your coat, let him have your cloak as well" (Mt. 5:40). These were strong words because the coat and the cloak were the most essential elements of clothing. The coat in Jesus' day was the long undergarment with sleeves. The cloak was worn over the coat; the poor used it as a coverlet at night. On the other hand, Jesus did not approve filing a suit. When asked to serve as a judge in litigation between brothers: "Teacher, bid my brother divide the inheritance with me," Jesus refused. "Man, who made me a judge or divider over you? . . . Take heed, and beware of all covetousness" (Lk. 12:13-15).

The most explicit teachings on litigation are found in Paul's first letter to the church at Corinth. "When one of you has a grievance against a brother, does he dare go to law before the unrighteous instead of the saints? . . . Are you incompetent to try trivial cases? . . . If then you have such cases, why do you lay them before those who are least esteemed by the church? I say this to your shame. Can it be that there is no man among you wise enough to decide between members of the brotherhood, but brother goes to law against brother, and that before unbelievers? To have lawsuits at all with one another is defeat for you. Why not rather suffer wrong? Why not rather be defrauded? But you yourselves wrong and defraud, and that even your own brethren" (1 Cor. 6:1-8).

Paul's teaching here seems to be limited to litigation within the Christian congregation itself. Most cases in modern business involve people outside the congregation and often outside the broader Christian fellowship as well. Often litigation involves people who are trying to avoid the payment of legitimate debts and are trying to take advantage of a businessman.

Jesus' teaching in the Sermon on the Mount, though given to his disciples, does not seem to involve relationships between one disciple and another. Jesus is not telling his disciples that they should not go to law and initiate a suit. He is assuming that they won't do that. Rather he is speaking about cases where others bring lawsuits against the Christian and where, apparently, the suit is demanding something for which the plaintiff has no justifiable claim.

Perhaps Jesus is using hyperbole here to emphasize that the Christian should willingly suffer loss if this will promote the Christian cause. But unjustifiable lawsuits are usually motivated by greed—sometimes of the most flagrant variety. Failure to contest such suits may only encourage more greed and so come under the condemnation that Jesus gave in Luke 12:14-15. Certainly Paul was frequently brought to court. He was careful to insist on being given his legal right and he ably defended these rights before the magistrates (Acts 16:37; 22:25; 23:3; 24:10; 25:8-12; 26:1-29). Indeed, the very defense of the legal right was at times used as a basis for an evangelistic appeal (Acts 26:29).

To make Matthew 5:40 a legalistic prohibition of all use of the courts for legal defense against wrongs makes no more sense to a twentieth-century businessman than to use another phrase from the Sermon on the Mount as a guide for business practice. Jesus said, "Therefore do not be anxious about tomorrow, for tomorrow will be anxious for itself"

(Mt. 6:34). The very essence of the entrepreneurial function in business is precisely the opposite of this. Engaging in business involves the bearing of risks. These risks must be reduced to reasonable proportions. But most of them relate to a careful assessment of contingencies which the future may bring.

I believe that Jesus did not intend to condemn careful calculations of future planning. Jesus' denunciation of anxiety about the future is, therefore, a criticism of the fear which paralyzes people from taking the risks necessary for any effective work. Jesus urged his followers to assume the risks of owning very little property (Lk. 14:33). He thus stands in judgment on our own propensities to take security in the possession of a multitude of things. But this does not rule out taking risks in a business enterprise where the entrepreneur is seeking to provide needed goods and services.

Jesus' teaching in the Sermon on the Mount and Paul's counsel to the church at Corinth are sometimes interpreted as ruling out all use of litigation by Christians. I would suggest rather that the following is a more appropriate interpretation. First, Christians should not normally use litigation to settle disputes with other Christians. Jesus prescribed a better method of solving such problems when he suggested first a private talk with the other Christian involved. If this doesn't resolve the problem, two or three other "witnesses" from the church should be brought into the discussion. If even this doesn't work, the entire church (assembly) should be involved (Mt. 18:15-18). Following this procedure does not completely rule out the use of the courts. Indeed, a judgment of the court might assist in coming to an amicable settlement—a settlement which may go considerably beyond the legal requirements because of Christian love and caring in the community.

We should explore alternatives to the courts, especially tools such as mediation and arbitration. Mediation involves the intervention of a third party for the purpose of resolving legal disputes between two parties. A mediator listens to each party's version of the facts; he then delineates for the parties the areas of agreement and disagreement. The mediator interprets the respective positions of the parties, sets any substantive and procedural ground rules which may be necessary, and seeks to discover and to suggest—but not to dictate—solutions to the dispute. A good mediator also helps to set and maintain a positive tone at the meeting. This is conducive to constructive efforts by both parties to achieve a settlement.

The purpose of mediation in the Christian community is to bring about the healing of a sinning Christian's broken relationship with God and with another Christian. Since the mediator acts as a catalyst to assist the disputing parties reach a settlement, rather than as a decision maker, the mediator is in a position to help reconcile the parties. The Christian mediator may even find it possible to assist one or both of the disputing parties to be reconciled with God.

Arbitration is more coercive than mediation but less so than litigation. In arbitration both parties to the dispute agree to the appointment of a third party who hears each side. At the time the arbitrator is chosen the disputants agree to accept the decision of the arbitrator as binding upon both parties. Since it involves the imposition of a decision, it is not as conducive to the healing of broken relationships as mediation would be. It is superior, however, to resorting to litigation.[17]

Second, where the Christian has been sued by someone outside the church, or where the Christian feels that someone is taking unfair advantage, litigation may be

necessary. But the spirit of Matthew 18 suggests that the
exact nature of the response should not be decided solely by
one Christian acting alone. We need the counsel of others in
the church.[18] Our unwillingness to ask for such counsel, and
at times the unwillingness of other members of the church to
give it, may be an indication of how far we have drifted from
being the kind of *church* Jesus intended. It may also be a
result of the large size of some of our business enterprises
and the numerous and complex issues which inevitably arise
from them. I will say more about this later.

Implicit Biblical Teachings on Business Ethics

In addition to the explicit teachings of the Bible on business ethics there are also Christian ethical principles which
are implicit. For example, in what type of business may a
Christian entrepreneur legitimately engage?

A Christian should not operate a house of prostitution or a
gambling casino even if such businesses are not explicitly
prohibited by Scripture. The Christian will also not produce
weapons of war nor weapon-related technology. The
military establishment has a huge budget and consequently
enormous purchasing power. It is tempting to any
entrepreneur to supply the military, but this temptation
should be forthrightly resisted by those who would follow
Jesus' way of peace. A statement adopted by a Study
Conference on Christian Community Relations in 1951 is
still valid: "That we give a better demonstration of our
unwillingness to profit through products of our labor or
capital which contribute directly to military operations or to
the destruction of property or life, or to participate in any
program which tends to promote ill will or hatred among
men or nations."[19]

The Bible teaches explicitly that drunkenness is a sin.

"And do not get drunk with wine, for that is debauchery"
(Eph. 5:18; Prov. 23:21; Joel 1:5; 1 Cor. 5:11; 1 Cor. 6:10;
Gal. 5:21). It is fair to assume that implicit in this teaching is
that the Christian entrepreneur should not engage in the
manufacture, sale, and distribution of strong drink.

I do not mean to imply that the Bible teaches total abstinence (1 Tim. 5:23). Jesus' first miracle as recorded by
John was the conversion of water into wine (Jn. 2:1-10), and
we are seriously weakening the power of the miracle when
we suggest that the wine produced had no alcoholic content.
Jesus was not an ascetic abstainer (Lk. 7:33-34). But it is an
unwarranted rationalization to infer that Jesus would have
supported the use of alcoholic beverages had he lived in the
emotionally charged atmosphere of the technologically complex twentieth century. I have already pointed out that
Jesus' teachings on the payment of interest need to be interpreted in the light of the fact that he lived in a precapi-
talistic economy. Similarly, I believe that were Jesus working
as an entrepreneur today he would neither manufacture, distribute, nor drink alcoholic beverages.

A half century ago America had national prohibition, and
the Christian churches largely supported it. The Christian
entrepreneur today faces the subtle temptation (stimulated
by relentless advertising campaigns) to regard abstinence as
a quaint, archaic, and unnecessary abridgement of the
"good life." Before yielding to this temptation the responsible Christian should be thoroughly acquainted with modern
evidence that there is no way of telling in advance whether
those who start to drink, even moderately, will not become
acute alcoholics. Those who drink and drive cars have a
good chance of becoming murderers.

The Bible also warns against the evils of ostentatious living (see, e.g., Amos 4:1-3). Implicit in this teaching is the additional warning that it is wrong to produce or to sell products that meet only the whimsical or luxury demands of the wealthy of our day. Quoting again from the 1951 Study Conference: "In view of the scriptural Mennonite emphasis upon simplicity of life ... Mennonite productive resources of land, labor, and capital [should] be engaged in the production of those goods and services which contribute more directly to the promotion of the gospel of Jesus Christ in the world and to the supplying of the necessities for sustaining and enriching life rather than the production of those things which weaken the mind or the body or which supply the trivial, superficial, or peripheral wants of man."[20] Precisely where to draw the line between legitimate necessities and ostentatious luxuries is not easy because there is a long continuum between obvious necessity and clearly frivolous luxury. The problem is a similar one to the problem of deciding on the Christian standard of living. I will say more about this in chapter five.

Advertising and Public Relations

As I noted above, the Bible speaks explicitly on questions of honesty. However, the Bible does not speak explicitly concerning advertising and sales promotion techniques. But certainly it is a fair conclusion that the explicit teachings on honesty implicitly apply to this area of business practice. For example, an advertisement for jewelry in the *New York Times*[21] by Bloomingdale's, a large department store in New York City, ran as follows: "For free spirits, our attention getters in 14K gold. Completely provocative. Wear them X-rated ... or paired with bikinis.... Get the picture? They accept everything ... and nothing. Are you ready to turn a few heads?" This advertisement to sell jewelry to wear with swimming suits or (by implication) in the raw was not the advertisement of a cheap burlesque theater in a city slum, but of a large department store.

Christians are naturally revolted against such excesses to achieve economic gain by the sale of products advertised to appeal to the prurient nature of man. But what about other advertising? Again we have a continuum that runs all the way from clearly unchristian advertising to the opposite pole of advertising that seeks to inform or to educate. The market system will work most effectively to keep prices at competitive levels if the public is informed of genuine bargains. But the Christian entrepreneur will have to decide with the help of the Holy Spirit and with the counsel of his fellow Christians just how far along the continuum to undesirable advertising he may legitimately go. The same criteria apply to sales promotion efforts other than direct advertising.

Public relations (PR) or the proper public image of an enterprise are closely related to advertising and should be conducted by following the same rules of honesty which we would expect would be evident in other aspects of Christian business practice. Some of these practices have received national and even international attention in recent years. The role of International Telephone and Telegraph (ITT) in the activities of the Central Intelligence Agency in Chile is an example of this. But the public image is also of importance to the relatively small enterprise, and the Christian manager of such an enterprise must ask himself whether he has dealt candidly with ethical problems which sometimes emerge. A recent article in the *Wall Street Journal* put the issue bluntly: "Talks with many PR agents indicate that ethical conflicts aren't uncommon in corporate PR departments. There are news releases designed to mislead the public. There are deliberate delays of bad news. There are lies to reporters and investors. There is stonewalling. There are coverups. There are sins of commission and sins of omission."[22]

Monopolistic Practices

I noted in chapter one that it is standard economic doctrine of laissez-faire economics that prices should be determined by the free operation of supply and demand in the market. In British and North American jurisprudence these economic doctrines have been fortified by common law principles against the "conspiracy to monopolize" or actions "in restraint of trade." In the United States these principles were codified in legislation such as the Sherman Anti-Trust Act of 1890 and the Clayton Act of 1914.

There is nothing explicit in the Bible which would clearly condemn such business practices. But an act by Jesus recorded in all four Gospels would seem to point in this direction. "And Jesus entered the temple of God and drove out all who sold and bought in the temple, and he overturned the tables of the money-changers and the seats of those who sold pigeons" (Mt. 21:12-13; Mk. 11:15-17; Lk. 19:45-46; Jn. 2:14-17). Jesus defended his action by an appeal to the prophecies of Isaiah and Jeremiah: " 'My house shall be called a house of prayer'; but you have made it a den of robbers" (Is. 56:7; Jer. 7:11).

The event was a propitious one. But it is unlikely that Jesus did this as a symbol of his opposition to the whole temple system. Jesus paid the half-shekel temple tax for himself and for Peter (Mt. 17:24-27). He asked a leper whom he had cured to bring to the priest the offering which Moses had prescribed (Mt. 8:4). But Jesus objected strenuously when a religious institution became blatantly commercialized. Furthermore, he protested against the fact that the money changers and merchants in the temple had an oppressive monopoly. They used their monopolistic position to charge unreasonable prices for the pigeons and animals they sold or to offer unreasonably poor exchange rates for the money they exchanged. The money changers gained at the expense of the poor who came to the temple to worship. Jesus' act, therefore, was clearly a sharp criticism of their abuse of monopoly power.

The small-scale Christian entrepreneur is usually not in a position to engage in monopolistic practices. Instead he probably comes nearer to the model of pure competition envisaged by the classical economists. But, regardless of size, the temptation to try to use monopolistic pricing is a strong one. Implicit in our biblical understanding is that this temptation is an invitation to sin.

Biblical Principles for Complex Modern Problems

In the discussion of explicit and implicit biblical teachings on business ethics, I have sometimes alluded to difficulties in applying these teachings to the complexities of the modern business situation. I will now turn to a consideration of some of the specific ethical dilemmas faced by the Christian entrepreneur today.

The Entrepreneur as an Agent for Others

Perhaps the most troublesome of all problems stems from the fact that many of today's entrepreneurs are not operating only or mainly for themselves; in many cases their acts may affect others more than they affect themselves. If the business is a sole proprietorship, the entrepreneur is acting largely for himself as sole owner and manager. But even in this simple form of business enterprise the entrepreneur's acts cannot be made in isolation from the effect they have on employees, suppliers, and customers. The partnership is a more complex form of business enterprise. The individual member of the partnership now must take into consideration his partners' interests (and ethical ideals) as well as his own.

The corporation is still more complex, and if the stock is widely held the entrepreneurial decisions of management are subject to the scrutiny of a large number of people, some of whom may have an economic interest in the decision as great or greater than the manager himself. Furthermore, the most significant decisions are not made by one person acting in isolation but are made by group consensus. Not all members of this group may be Christians. If Christians, not all may have the same understanding of Christian ethics.

The problems arising from being an agent for others are clearly some of the most critical areas of concern for Christian entrepreneurs. Those with whom I have talked have often confirmed that their experiences in "going public" have not been good ones. Faithfulness to biblical norms suggests that, as businesses expand, those who are drawn into the business should share the Christian ideals of the original partners or stockholders—not merely provide them with additional capital.

Paul warned the Christians at Corinth: "Do not be mismated with unbelievers. For what partnership have righteousness and iniquity? Or what fellowship has light with darkness? What accord has Christ with Belial? Or what has a believer in common with an unbeliever?" (2 Cor. 6:14-15). The King James Version uses the words "unequally yoked" in translating this passage, and this gives rise to a Christian doctrine sometimes referred to as the "prohibition of the unequal yoke." Daniel Kauffman stated that it applies to business, though he did not specify precisely how.[23] It has also been used to suggest that membership in secret orders is un-Christian. Because Corinth was such a palpably pagan city, it seems evident that Paul was warning Christians against forming close ties with pagans. Certainly it rules out the defilement of the body through unlawful sex relations (2 Cor. 7:1). Christians should not enter into marriage relationships with pagans, but Paul had already advised the members of the church at Corinth not to divorce pagan spouses (1 Cor. 7:12-16). But in this same passage Paul also suggested that an amicable separation may be desirable.

It seems unlikely that Paul intended his warning against the unequal yoke be used to forbid necessary business relations or ordinary friendliness with the members of the pagan community. Jesus established the example of associating with tax collectors and sinners. This scandalized the religious community of his day, no doubt in part from the fact that Jesus' association with them involved eating with them (Mt. 9:10-13) or drinking water from a common vessel (Jn. 4:7-9), both of which implied an intimacy repugnant to a strict Jew. But in both of these situations Jesus was using his association with the pagan community as a means of sharing the good news.

The sharing of the good news is an opportunity open to Christians in all ages; it is incumbent on the earnest follower of Christ to rise to meet the challenges of these opportunities. The problem is, of course, that in making these associations we are tempted to allow our lives to be conformed to the standards of the pagan world, rather than attempt to transform it. In the business world, as we act on behalf of others, do we assume they live by a lower ethical standard thereby justifying a lower standard for ourselves? Or are we going to try to maintain the ethical standards to which we believe Christ has called us?

CHAPTER 4

Christian Ethics in Business: Specific Applications

In this chapter I would like to illustrate the general questions I raised in chapter three by reference to some specific business policy decisions. One of the most important decisions a businessman makes is the pay scale for his laborers. Wages constitute approximately 80 percent of the total national income; this means that they usually constitute the single most important expense of operating a business. Some businesses involve the further processing or the sale of products which already involve many labor costs; in these cases a good share of the total labor bill may already have been paid by the firms which supply the goods processed or sold. In such businesses the manager's direct control over wage rates is greatly reduced because wage decisions have already been made by the supplier.

The pay scale for workers is important not only because it is the major cost for Christian entrepreneurs but because it is usually the *only* source of income for the workers. Jesus said:

"The laborer deserves his wages" (Lk. 10:7). In his severe criticism of the rich James wrote that they had "kept back by fraud" the "wages of the laborers who mowed your fields" and that the suffering of these workers had resulted in "cries" which "reached the ears of the Lord of hosts" (Jas. 5:4). The Levitical code required that wages be paid promptly: "The wages of a hired servant shall not remain with you all night until the morning" (Lev. 19:13). The Old Testament prophets also expressed deep concern. Jeremiah pronounced a "Woe to him . . . who makes his neighbor serve him for nothing, and does not give him his wages" (Jer. 22:13). Similarly, Malachi prophesied against "those who oppress the hireling in his wages" (Mal. 3:5; see also Ezek. 29:18-19 and Hag. 1:6).

To the modern businessman, faced with ever increasing demands from his workers for higher pay, the biblical teachings may seem quaint and anachronistic. In biblical times many workers were slaves and received no monetary wages at all. The presence of a substantial slave class in the Hebrew economy must have severely depressed the monetary wages of the free workers. Today, by contrast, labor in many industries is well organized, and the workers' drives for unionization are protected by legislation, the National Labor Relations Board, and by the courts. Plumbers in Pittsburgh were reported to have a union scale of $22.75 per hour in 1978 and jobs requiring less than an hour of time are charged for the full hour.[1]

Today nearly half of all workers in manufacturing enterprises are unionized. In some branches of manufacturing the percentage is much higher—well over 80 percent. In other branches, for example printing, the percentage of workers who are unionized is much less. The relative importance of production workers in manufacturing, mining, and transport (groups historically most prone to join unions) is declining. As a result the percentage of the total labor force in unions is declining in the United States. About 27 percent of nonfarm workers are unionized today as compared to 31 percent in 1960. On the other hand nearly 80 percent of the workers in the contract construction field are members of unions. In highly unionized businesses it is understandable if the entrepreneur today feels that the real ethical issue is how the employer can be protected from the unreasonable wage requests of monopolistically organized workers rather than how the worker can be protected from the rapacity of the employer.

Ideally, the labor-management relationship should be one of mutual support. The worker should realize that the businessman has provided the capital and the entrepreneurial skills which have provided the job for the worker. On the other hand, the entrepreneur should recognize that his capital cannot be productive unless workers render their services. This ideal is, of course, sometimes achieved. But in many cases labor and management have come to view each other as hostile opponents. The worker's mind tends to magnify the profits earned by the entrepreneur and to view profits as money which really should have gone to the worker in the form of higher wages. On the other hand, employers have felt that workers' demands for higher wages have been unreasonable. They feel that workers do not realize that when profits are inadequate there is insufficient capital formation to make the worker's job secure or to provide additional jobs for the young people who are newcomers to the labor market. Instead of mutual support and understanding between management and labor, there are often feelings of hostility and distrust on both sides.

Higher wages for workers do not always result in lower

profits for the entrepreneur. Perhaps instead they mean that the worker will work with greater diligence. Higher wage rates in general may provide workers with the purchasing power to buy more goods and thus increase the general level of economic activity. It was said years ago that Henry Ford felt it was "good business" to pay his workers $5 a day because they needed adequate wages to buy the model T Fords they were manufacturing. Similarly, Ford adopted a five-day working week so his workers would have the leisure time to drive their Fords. Higher wages and shorter hours will not result in lower profits if the entrepreneur is in a position to pass on higher wages to the consumer in the form of higher prices. This may be particularly the case when the employer has at least a partial monopolistic position or where, as in the case of the defense contractor, he is operating on a "cost-plus" basis.

Whether the effect of the higher wages is to cause inflation (thereby hurting the consumer), reduce profits (thereby hurting the owners and managers), or cause technological unemployment (thereby giving higher incomes for some at the expense of the unemployment of others)—the decision of the level of wages to be paid is probably the most agonizing one faced by many Christian entrepreneurs. The decision would be a relatively easy one if there were a clearly established market rate of wages. The employer could then pay this rate of wage without argument. His position would be similar to the position of the Christian bake shop operator who simply pays the market price for the flour and other ingredients of the baked goods he manufactures.

But unfortunately there is no such clearly established price of labor (wage). If the community in which the entrepreneur is operating is a small one, there may be only two or three employers who provide jobs for most of the workers in the community. If the rates of pay offered by these employers are too low, theoretically the workers could leave the community and go elsewhere to find jobs which are more remunerative. Certainly some of this type of migration goes on. But we have to reckon with what the economist calls the "immobility of labor." There are ties of family, ties of local church congregation, special relationships which children have developed with their school chums or peer groups. Families in which both husband and wife work outside the home also have an immobility which stems from the fact that one spouse hesitates to move as a result of inadequate pay when the other spouse has a job which offers both personal self-fulfillment and a good wage. All of these complications militate against the establishment of a free market price for labor that will provide the employer with ready bench marks for his own wage policy.

The problem is made still more difficult by the fact that wage rates often have reflected traditions rather than economic realities or Christian justice. When we hear that plumbers in Pittsburgh are being paid $22.75 an hour, or that coal miners reach a wage settlement with coal operators for pay of $11.40, we instinctively feel that there is an element of immorality in asking for such pay. On the other hand medical doctors or other professional people may earn more than this and we accept it as a matter of course.

Part of the reason for the high pay of professional people is that they must have completed a long and costly period of education before they are able to earn any income at all. But the disparity is too great to be accounted for solely by differences in costs of education or apprenticeship. It partly reflects the tradition that white collar and professional pay should be greater than blue collar wages. But it may also reflect the fact that the number of qualified professional persons is not adequate to meet the demand we place on their services. The Soviet Union has nearly twice as many doctors relative to its population than the United States. The pay for Soviet doctors is near the bottom of their pay scale, a monthly income of "$133-173, less than the average factory workers."[2]

Part of the reason for the high pay being given to plumbers and coal miners is that their work is physically demanding and often unpleasant or even unhealthful. The coal miner may suffer a premature death because of black lung disease or of explosions or cave-ins in the mines. Cleaning a clogged toilet is not a pleasant task. The Pittsburgh plumber who earned $22.75 an hour is said to have opened a clogged sewer on New Year's eve—a time which may have been just about as inconvenient for him as the obstetrician faces when a baby is born at 3:00 a.m. What is a reasonable remuneration for the inconvenient work schedule, the unpleasant task, the shorter working life? Jobs that involve tedium, nerve strain, seasonal layoff, irregular employment, or low social prestige are less attractive to people. Even though by tradition such jobs have also often been poorly paid, it does not seem unreasonable that higher rates be paid to compensate for some of these special problems.

Provisions for Retirement of Workers

In a predominantly rural society relatively little thought was given for the needs of retired workers. The average lifespan was shorter in those days and many workers died from infectious diseases or accidents before they reached what we today would consider a "retirement age." If they did live beyond the biblical "threescore and ten," they may have resided in a small house on the farm adjacent to the home of one of their children. Perhaps they continued to contribute something to the economy of the household by working in the garden or by doing other chores—as their strength permitted. But today we have an urban society. Advances in medicine have meant a much larger proportion of our population reaches "threescore and ten, and even . . . fourscore." Average life expectancy in the United States advanced from 47 years in 1900 to 74 years in 1979. Many of the higher paid jobs in manufacturing, construction, or mining are too physically demanding to be performed effectively by persons who at age 65 are still in good health but are not as agile or as strong as they were at 35. What responsibilities does the Christian entrepreneur face in providing job security for workers?

The strong tradition in Japan of lifelong job security is strikingly different from the United States and Canada. Although some changes are now being made in Japanese industry, traditionally young workers assume, when they take their first job with a business firm, that they will continue with that firm throughout their entire working life. If business falls off fewer (or perhaps no) new workers will be hired, but those who already have their jobs will keep them.

In contrast the typical North American worker may move frequently from employer to employer—especially in the early years of his employment. But as the worker approaches 45 to 50 years of age, it becomes extremely difficult to move to another job. To do so may mean having to move from a more-skilled to a less-skilled type of work. What responsibilities should the Christian entrepreneur take in bearing at least part of the burden that is placed on the worker who loses his job because of technological changes that could not have been foreseen a decade or two ago? Certainly Christian compassion must be exercized here as in all phases of life.

Many business people today try to meet some of these

problems in part by establishing pension funds for their workers. They supplement these plans with health and accident insurance schemes, under government or private auspices. In fact, "fringe benefits" have become a substantial part of the wage payments made by many employers today. For American industry generally these benefits constituted 16 percent of the payroll in 1947. Twenty years later they were nearly 30 percent and today they are over 35 percent of the payroll. Benefits cost the employer about $4,000 per year for each worker. However, they tend to be smaller, on the average, in businesses having only a few nonunion workers. The Christian entrepreneur should examine his own practices carefully to determine whether he is being fair with his workers in fringe benefits as well as whether the basic rates of pay are adequate.

Pricing Policies

In the Middle Ages the Catholic Church decreed that workers were to be paid a "just wage." We have just examined ways in which this is still the responsibility of the Christian entrepreneur today. But the church also asked that in the sale of goods the price charged should be a "just price." This also is a reasonable rule for the Christian entrepreneur to follow today. But what is a "just price"? Here we must differentiate between the situation faced by producers who are operating under what economists call conditions of perfect competition and those who are operating under imperfect competition, oligopoly (control of market by a few producers) or monopoly (control of market by one producer).

Let us take up the situation of perfect competition first because it is easiest to understand. Perfect competition is said to exist where there are so many producers competing in the market that the action of no one producer has any appreciable effect on the market. Furthermore the product produced is a homogeneous or standardized product. For example, number two soft red wheat grown by one farmer is identical to the same grade of wheat grown by any other farmer. In such a situation the market price is determined entirely by the impersonal forces of supply and demand. The individual producer has absolutely no control over the price. He does, of course, have some control over the quantity of goods he offers for sale.

If a farmer does not like the current market price of wheat, he may be able to withhold his own crop from the market for a time in the hope that market prices will improve. But there are so many wheat farmers that the action of one farmer in withholding his wheat crop will not make even a little ripple in the market price for wheat. Furthermore, he may not be in a position to withhold his wheat because of storage costs, the interest cost of holding such a large inventory, or because he is unwilling to bear the risk that the future price may actually be lower than the present price. For these reasons it appears that there is no ethical problem in pricing by the individual producer operating under conditions of perfect competition.

But the perfectly competitive market is becoming increasingly rare in modern business life. Outside of agricultural production imperfect competition, oligopoly, or monopoly are the usual types of markets. We can think of these conditions as existing on a continuum. At the one extreme is perfect competition where there are so many producers of a product that the action of no one producer has any effect on the market. At the other extreme is absolute monopoly where there is only one seller. This is even more rare, although a number of years ago the Aluminum Company of

America virtually had such an absolute monopoly. Oligopoly is more common. Here not one, but a few, producers dominate the market. We can easily think of examples of oligopoly in products like automobiles, soft drinks, cigarettes, and the like.

Imperfect competition is still more prevalent. In such markets there are more than just a few producers (as there are in oligopoly); but there are still not enough producers for the action of a single producer to have no influence on the market (as in perfect competition). On the continuum from one polarity of absolute monopoly to the other polarity of perfect competition, imperfect competition would be approximately in the middle. Some elements of competition are present; some elements of monopoly are involved. In fact, some economists have used the term "monopolistic competition" to describe the situation.

For our purposes the significant point about imperfect competition is that the seller has some control over the price of the product he sells. His price dare not be too much above the price charged by his competitors or he will suffer a loss of sales. Furthermore, his product (for example toothpaste), though similar to that of his competitors, is not identical to it. As a result he may advertise the product to call attention to its superior qualities; if the advertising is convincing to a significant number of consumers, the seller may be able to charge more without suffering an undue loss of sales.

It is precisely here that ethical problems emerge. How honest is the advertising? Does the product really possess the superiority which the advertising claims? Does the advertiser resort to appeals of dubious morality to promote the sales? It takes only a quick review of national advertising in newspapers, magazines, TV, and billboards to demonstrate that the appeal is often not to the inherent worth of the product, but to such things as sex appeal, snob appeal, and conspicuous consumption.

Church theologians of the Middle Ages who advised their people to charge a "just price" were unaware of the intricacies of modern economic analysis in the marketplace. But as one reads their writings it would appear that they were aiming at a price which we would call today the equivalent of the cost of production. In other words the price should be adequate to cover the cost of the materials, a just wage to the workers, and a reasonable return to the entrepreneur for his services in bearing the responsibilities and risks in the business enterprise.

It is obviously difficult to apply this simplistic analysis to the infinitely more complex business situations of today. Although today's products are still material and are made up of clearly recognizable costs of production, the demand for the product is often based on psychological or other noneconomic factors. Many items are produced in which entrepreneurs recognize that failure or success in the marketplace are equally possible. When the producer has failed to assess consumer demand accurately, the selling price will have to be below (perhaps much below) the costs of production. Nevertheless, the medieval rule of "just price" should serve Christian entrepreneurs today as a reminder that pricing policies must always involve ethical as well as economic considerations. Christians will want to analyze their own pricing policies in the light of these principles.

Pollution of the Environment

In producing "goods" entrepreneurs sometimes inevitably produce some "bads" along with them. Sometimes the smoke and sulphur dioxide of coal-fired boilers begrimes the paint on houses, dirties the clothes on wash lines, tarnishes or corrodes metal ware, and leads to lung cancer or other human diseases. River water used for industrial cooling may have its temperature increased so that fish are no longer so abundant. Or, worse still, industrial wastes disposed of in rivers and lakes may contaminate water used for human consumption. This not only endangers the health of the public but it also impairs the usefulness of these God-given resources for recreational enjoyment.

In recent years many governments have imposed standards on businesses in an effort to reduce environmental pollution. But at times these standards have proved to be very difficult to enforce. The problem is that adhering to the standards adds significantly to the costs of production. This makes it difficult for businesses who obey the rules to compete with those who violate them. Capital investment in pollution-control equipment may require funds which the businessman was hoping to use to make his production more "efficient." Efforts made to avoid environmental pollution should be regarded as legitimate a cost of production as materials, labor, and other overhead costs. Therefore, the cost of pollution control measures should also be included in formulating pricing policy. If consumers are not willing to bear these real costs, they should be willing to get along without buying the product.

In any event Christian entrepreneurs should not contribute to the pollution of the environment. The environment is a part of the earth which the Lord made and called "good." Just as Christian farmers will carefully husband the soil which they farm and will attempt to have it be just as fertile for their children as it was when they received it, so also Christian manufacturers will be good stewards of the environment surrounding their factories.

Corporate Gifts for Social Welfare Purposes

One of the joys of being in business is that the income earned is available for supporting the church and other useful causes. I want to discuss this point at some length in chapter six. Now I want to consider the problem that arises when the business person is not a sole proprietor but is rather associated with others in a partnership or corporate forms of business organization. Here there is more than one owner; in a corporation there may be many owners. When a corporation decides to give money for social welfare purposes, the person or persons making the decisions are not only giving their own money; they are also giving the money of other stockholders who may not agree with the purposes of the gift. Some economists, such as Professor Friedman of the University of Chicago, have argued that all such gifts by corporations are, therefore, immoral. They would not permit corporations to make charitable gifts. Instead they advocate that the corporation distribute the money which it might otherwise donate to charity to the stockholders individually. The individual stockholders would then make their own private decisions on whether they will personally give to charity, and if so, how much.

The problem is not a serious one for Christian entrepreneurs who operate relatively small-scale partnerships or corporations. Presumably in such cases decisions need not rest on one person or a small inner group of management, but could be made at a stockholders' meeting in which all owners have an effective voice. This is another good reason to avoid broad ownership of a company. But even in some relatively small corporations, the stock is too widely held to permit this kind of consensus. Even in these cases, however, an ethical case can be made for corporate gifts for social purposes. The argument is essentially the same as the argument for taxation of corporation profits by the government. Obviously, such taxes do not really rest on the corporation itself (for the corporation is an impersonal fictional person), but rather upon the owners of the corporation (in the form of lower profits), or the consumers of the products produced (in the form of higher prices). It should not be considered wrong to give even if corporate gifts reduce profits.

The corporation is itself a creature of society and it has a responsibility to society. The corporation today is such a ubiquitous institution that we sometimes forget that it came on the scene very recently in the long span of human history. Early corporations were considered to be so unusual that each corporation had to have a charter granted by the king or a special act of Parliament in England or by a special act of the legislature in the United States. Adam Smith, writing in 1776, did not even think of the corporate form of business enterprise as being appropriate for manufacturing. It is only since the middle of the nineteenth century that corporate charters were made available to all who would follow a certain prescribed procedure. It is only in the present century that the corporate form of business enterprise has become truly widespread. Since it accepts a benefit of society (the corporate charter), it is not inappropriate that the corporation should return benefits to society whether in the form of involuntary taxes or of voluntary corporate gifts.

Hiring Minority and Disadvantaged Persons

When Christian entrepreneurs employ workers they should give careful consideration to their responsibility to secure the rights of minority peoples who live within North America. These problems also exist in some European countries such as England, the Netherlands, and France. England has a sizable minority population of persons who migrated from former British colonies in the West Indies, Asiatic India, and Africa. The Netherlands is host to people migrating from the East Indies; France has its Algerian minority.

Special historic factors have exacerbated minority problems in the United States and Canada. Long before the first European settlers came to these shores, native Americans were living here (through historical accident misnamed "Indians"). The early settlers took by force the lands they occupied and the hunting and fishing rights they enjoyed. European immigrants killed some of the native Americans and they placed those who survived on "reservations." Thus they hoped they would not constitute a "threat" to the invading European conquerers whose "manifest destiny" was to occupy the lands which the Indians once claimed as their own. It is estimated that today there are fewer than a million of these people in the United States, but their population has more than doubled in the last thirty years.

The black population is much larger—almost 23 million persons according to the 1970 United States Census. Today it is probably more than 27 million. These people, often called Afro-Americans, are the descendants of persons brought to the United States by force to serve as slave laborers. Since the majority of them were brought here in the seventeenth and eighteenth centuries, they have also lived in North America much longer than the millions of immigrants who came here from Europe in the nineteenth and early twentieth centuries.

Latin Americans constitute another large, though somewhat less readily identifiable, group. The Census Bureau reports that there were nearly 11 million of these people in the United States in 1974. About 60 percent came to the

United States from Mexico. The others came largely from Puerto Rico, Cuba, and other Latin American countries.

A common characteristic of all of these minority groups is that they have been subjected to discrimination—in employment, in rates of pay, and in admission to educational institutions and sometimes to public facilities. In recent years the federal government has attempted to correct some of the worst of these abuses through legislation. But current statistics indicate that legislation has not eliminated the problems it was designed to solve. Unemployment rates among blacks, for example, are currently twice as high as for whites; unemployment among black teenagers is three times that of whites.[3] Twenty-five years ago the family incomes of nonwhites averaged about half of those of white families. By the middle 1970s this fraction had climbed to about three fifths. Although this represents some progress, it is clear that the progress has been very slow.

Sir Arthur Lewis, a distinguished black economist from the West Indies who served on the faculty of Princeton University and is recognized as one of the world's leading economists, has written: "The black problem is that while we are 11 percent of the [U.S.] population, we have only 2 percent of the jobs at the top, 4 percent of the jobs in the middle, and are forced into 16 percent of the jobs at the bottom." Andrew F. Brimmer, distinguished professor at the Harvard Graduate School of Business Administration and director on many corporate boards, was the first black ever to serve on the Board of Governors of the Federal Reserve System. He stated, "I am personally convinced that the most promising path of economic opportunity for Negroes lies in full participation in an integrated national economy. This holds for Negroes who want to be businessmen as well as for everyone else."

Another large group (so large, in fact, that they cannot be called a minority because they constitute more than half of the total population) which has been widely discriminated against is women. A woman who has the same amount of schooling as a man, the same parental background, and an identical IQ or other aptitude or test scores, will receive on the average only about 70 percent of the pay which would go to a man of similar abilities and background. Furthermore, only a few are likely to rise to positions of executive leadership in business organizations.

What are the responsibilities of Christian entrepreneurs in the face of this kind of injustice? The easy answer is that they should do better than their nonchristian competitors are doing. This is an obvious truth, but it is too vague an answer and too easy a way out. We cannot really achieve justice by being less "unjust" than others. We follow one who taught "unless your righteousness exceeds that of the scribes and Pharisees, you will never enter the kingdom of heaven" (Mt. 5:20). We believe with the Apostle Paul that "there is neither Jew nor Greek, there is neither slave nor free, there is neither male nor female; for you are all one in Christ Jesus" (Gal. 3:28).

It is just as important for Christian businesspeople to operate on these biblical principles in their own businesses as it is to adhere strictly to other biblical requirements such as honesty. This means that we will pay women and members of minority groups equal pay for equal work. We will give these people equal opportunities for promotion to positions of responsibility and leadership and equal assurance of job security as compared with all other employees. I do not mean to underestimate the difficulties of carrying out this principle in practice. It is costly to pay our women employees equal pay for equal work when our competitors do not do so. But it may also be costly to follow practices of strict honesty when our competitors do not do so. The problem is that we tend to make an absolute of some biblical ethical standards such as honesty, but we take less seriously other biblical ethical standards such as the equality of races or sexes. God's standards of justice do not permit this selective type of ethical behavior.

Employing the Handicapped and the Ex-Prisoner

There are more than 23 million handicapped persons in the United States. This means that more than one person in every ten has some kind of disabling, or partially disabling, condition. Persons with heart trouble, arthritis and rheumatism, visual impairments, hypertension, and mental or nervous disorders are examples of handicapped people. Disabled war veterans constitute another significant group of handicapped. Although more than one-fourth of these people are 65 years of age or older and would normally be retired anyway, more than 8 million disabled men and more than 7 million disabled women are under 65 years of age; many of these persons would be on the labor market if it were not for their disability.[4]

It is difficult to say how many of these people could be employed if proper working conditions were available for them and proper supervision given. But certainly many of them could be. In order to make them employable special instructions may be required, a shorter working day may be necessary, special transportation facilities may need to be provided, they may need to sit down at work, ramps and elevators may need to replace stairways.

Some handicapped people are employed in "sheltered workshops." A 1938 American law excluded blind and other severely handicapped persons from the usual wage and hour regulations which apply to other workers. More than 100 workshops employing at least 6,000 blind workers were established to employ blind workers to produce, assemble, or package various products. They are often paid at piece-rate wages. But since they are "sheltered" from the wage-hour laws, they often earn much less than the minimum wage. Many workers earn less than $1 an hour (some get only carfare) and they have no fringe benefits or job security. "Frequent layoffs often hold their annual incomes below $1, 500. Administrators of the workshops, by contrast, often receive salaries in the $50,000 range, with substantial benefits."[5] Some of the products of the sheltered workshops are sold to the federal government or to state governments. Some of the workshops are under contract with big companies like General Electric, Procter and Gamble, and American Telephone and Telegraph. The *Wall Street Journal* reporters who investigated the workshops concluded that the workers were subjected to unfair advantage.[6]

Sheltered workshops established by a Canadian missionary in France (called in French "Centre d'aide par le travail) offer a striking contrast to this sorry story. Robert Witmer established the first of these at Chatenay-Malabry, a suburb of Paris. Many of the workers there have limited IQs and often subnormal motor skills as well. However, under close supervision they are able to perform such routine operations as reassembling after each flight headsets used by passengers on Air France. They also put in the rivets on ring binders and engage in other routinized operations. The workers are paid at their rate of productivity but the Ministry of Social Welfare of the French Government provides a subsidy which brings their total income up to the level of a living wage. The Ministry has also provided help for transportation costs.

Because of the success of the workshop at Chatenay-Malabry, a second workshop was established at Haute-feuille, another suburb about 35 kilometers east of Paris. Here dormitories were built because some of the handicapped workers do not have an adequate home base or family life. The subsidy provided by the Ministry of Social Welfare will gradually help to amortize the capital investment in the dormitories. After gaining experience in work, some workers have been able to secure jobs in local industries. Some have become sufficiently mature to live independently in society. By challenging the French government to provide subsidy payments for such workshops, rather than offering mere welfare handouts to the handicapped people, Witmer has been instrumental in influencing the French Ministry to have similar workshops in every department (roughly equivalent to a U.S. state) of France. Prior to the opening of the first Mennonite program at Chatenay, there were only two others in all of France.[7]

Witmer has shown what an entrepreneur-turned-missionary can do in France. Aren't there Christian entrepreneurs in the United States and Canada who could be similarly creative on this side of the Atlantic? Governmental help for some types of endeavors is available, but the individual employer still needs to take some initiative and, in some cases, needs to take on added financial responsibility as well. But think of the tremendous contributions these efforts will make to those who are disabled. Their sense of self-worth will have been enhanced and they will see in the action of the Christian employer some of the compassion which Jesus displayed toward the disadvantaged of his day.

More than 300,000 persons are sent to prison each year.[8] Nearly two thirds of these people are discharged each year and the average time served is less than 20 months. A prison record is also a form of disability which effectively prevents many ex-prisoners from securing gainful employment. As a result, many feel driven to repeat the same kinds of crime which sent them to jail in the first instance. It is also probable that the parole rate would be considerably higher if parole officers thought there was a genuine opportunity for the paroled prisoner to secure gainful employment.

In Jesus' vivid sermon on the last judgment, he says, "I was hungry and you gave me food, I was thirsty and you gave me drink, I was a stranger and you welcomed me, I was naked and you clothed me, I was sick and you visited me, I was in prison and you came to me" (Mt. 25:35). The organized relief programs of the Christian churches have done much to feed the hungry and clothe the naked. We exert special efforts to welcome the stranger who comes to our church services, and individually we try to be friendly to our new neighbors. We either visit those who are sick (especially if they are hospitalized) or send them "get well soon" notes. We have begun to do a few things to show our compassion for those who are in prison. But if we are to carry out Jesus' mission of bringing "release to the captives" (Lk. 4:18), we need to make special effort to enable the ex-prisoner to become a normal part of community life. For many, the most important aspect of this would be the provision of employment.

The provision of employment for the physically disadvantaged or disabled may require that the employer make a special investment in training or in physical facilities. The employer takes some special kinds of risks in the employment of the ex-prisoner. As I noted in chapter one, risk bearing is an essential entrepreneurial function. The economic reward for successful risk bearing is profit. It is not at all certain that successfully bearing the risks of employing the ex-prisoner will add to the profits on the bottom line. But they will contribute substantially to general welfare because it costs society more to maintain a convict in prison than to educate him in a university. Still more important, they will meet the special challenge which Christian entrepreneurs face in making their faith relevant to their daily tasks.

Special Ethical Problems Faced in the Large Enterprise

Most of the ethical issues I have discussed thus far are relevant to all kinds of business enterprise, regardless of size. A few of them (such as pricing problems) pose more difficult ethical decisions in larger enterprises. Similarly, the ethical dilemmas facing managers of businesses having many stockholders with widely differing ethical standards and sensitivities are likely to be more troublesome the larger the enterprise becomes. But there are some other business practices of certain large corporations which I will now consider.

Trade with South Africa

One of the issues which must be faced is the use of the power of the corporation to attain certain desired social or political goals. An example of this would be the attempt to influence the racist policies of the government of the Union of South Africa. This is an issue which is much too large for any one business to cope with. Perhaps it is an issue on which the entrepreneur, while feeling sympathy with oppressed blacks, feels it is inappropriate to interfere. But one cannot be really neutral in matters of this kind. If the opportunity for trade is present and is taken, the economy of South Africa is strengthened. If it is not taken, the economy is weakened.

Discrimination against blacks is a serious problem in the United States; it is a much more serious problem in the Union of South Africa. There rigorous separation of races and assertions of white supremacy have long been accepted as logical and "natural." Following the official adoption of a policy of apartheid as the dominant Nationalist Party platform in 1948, it is a political issue as well. The officially stated purpose of apartheid is to perpetuate the domination of the country by its white minority. African Negroes (the Bantu) comprise about 70 percent of the entire population. These, together with the Asiatic (Indian) and the Coloured (mulattoes) have virtually no national political and economic rights. Instead they are set apart on reserved lands, their movements are severely regulated and restricted, and ordinary social interaction with whites is strictly forbidden.

Most of the land in South Africa, including the highly valuable mineral areas and the best sections of the cities, is reserved for the whites. The Bantu are not permitted to vote, or to hold property, or to work outside of designated areas. In urban centers they must always carry identification papers and they are subject to rigorous curfew regulations. Their rates of pay are only a small fraction of that earned by whites. These substandard wages have contributed to making South Africa a prosperous place for its white population. In addition, many large American banks have made loans to South African businesses, some American corporations have established subsidiaries or branch factories or in other ways have made direct investments in South Africa, and many American businesses have had trading relationships there.

What attitude should the Christian entrepreneur take toward having business relationships of any kind with South Africa? For many small businesses this will be no problem because the scope of their operations do not extend to South

Africa. But where such relationships are a possibility, a prior consideration should be a careful investigation of the kind of business practices being followed by the businesses with whom one is proposing to deal. Most Christian entrepreneurs would not think it appropriate to engage in business with a manufacturer or distributor of alcoholic beverages nor to produce or sell gambling equipment for a casino. On these issues following Paul's injunction to "abstain from all appearance of evil" (1 Thess. 5:22, KJV) is accepted as our Christian duty.

We need to develop our consciences to the point that we recognize that racism is also a sin—one which often has more devastating consequences than other sins that we are inclined to view more seriously. There is racism in the United States—so much so that we must be humble about it and seek to correct it. But the institutionalized and thoroughgoing racism of the Union of South Africa is more pervasive and more flagrant. It is appropriate for the Christian entrepreneur to witness against it by suspending business relationships with businesses there. At the same time we should witness to these people in our own business practices by following the teaching of One who said, "And men will come from east and west, and from north and south, and sit at table in the kingdom of God" (Lk. 13:29).

In my zeal to call attention to the flagrant problems of racism in the Union of South Africa, I am admittedly guilty of oversimplification. There are many powerful counterarguments. Some observers feel that if Americans do not trade directly with South Africa, the trade will go on anyway through third countries. This means that South Africans are not actually being encouraged to change their apartheid policies; instead, by making them martyrs or pariahs we are actually strengthening the determination and will of the party in power. There are other complex questions. Should we stop all trade—even including life-saving drugs and school supplies? If we take an absolutist position toward the evil in South Africa, what should we do about the less publicized evils in countries such as Argentina or Chile? Certainly we should be sensitive to all of these problems and formulate our own answers from an informed awareness.

Bribery to Stimulate Sales

Very large corporations make sales which total not just millions, but hundreds of millions of dollars. With the potential for sales being this high, the temptation to make bribes in order to consummate a sale increases. The activities of the Lockheed Company are a much-publicized example of this in recent years. Bribes paid by this company to secure sales of aircraft in Japan were an important contributor to the fall of the Tanaka government there. It has also been alleged that a member of the royal household in the Netherlands was the beneficiary of this corporation's largesse.

But Lockheed is by no means the only company which has been involved. The *Wall Street Journal* reported: "It was July 1971, and Howard Kauffmann was about to face one of the most difficult decisions in his life. Mr. Kauffmann was then president of an Exxon Corp. unit based in London. . . . The issue confronting Mr. Kauffmann was whether to approve a $700,000 'contribution' in Italy—which some investigators consider an outright bribe—in connection with the settlement of a $30 million Italian tax claim against Esso Italiana. In the end, and with great reluctance, he approved the payment. Today Mr. Kauffmann is president of the parent Exxon Corp. in New York and in line to become chairman and chief executive of the corporation."[9]

Another news report stated, "A sordid chapter in the history of United Brands Co. ended yesterday when the major food concern pleaded guilty to charges that it conspired to pay a $2.5 million bribe to a prominent Honduran official. . . . Judge William Conner . . . immediately fined United Brands $15,000, the maximum sentence. . . . According to the Department of Justice, the United Brands case is the third criminal prosecution in recent months involving payments to foreign officials by U.S. concerns. In March, Williams Co. pleaded guilty to charges of bribing officials of an unnamed foreign government to get work permits for expatriate personnel. The Oklahoma-based fertilizer and energy conglomerate received a criminal fine of $21,000 and was assessed $177,000 as a civil penalty for violating currency laws. In April, Control Data Corp. pleaded guilty to bribing unnamed foreign officials to obtain approval of sales of computer products to agencies of that government. Its criminal fine totaled $1.1 million."[10]

A common defense of this kind of illegal activity is that it is the "normal way of doing business" in many countries—almost a way of life which should be accepted as other cultural differences are tolerated. Often the country where the fines are paid have incredibly corrupt one-party governments. If American businessmen do not pay the fines, less scrupulous businessmen from other countries will willingly do so to gain the business.

This is an intolerable violation of Christian ethical standards. The payment of these bribes clearly perpetuates the vast inequalities in the distribution of wealth and income in these countries and further thwarts their sound economic development. Sometimes the bribes are not large ones to high officials of government but small bribes to the petty officials in the customs or tax office. The governments of some foreign countries pay these bureaucrats substandard wages because they know that the wages they pay will be augmented by the bribes they regularly receive. Failure to "pay off" these small-scale officials will mean that business relationships are interrupted by interminable delays. In some cases it is simply impossible to engage in business at all without following the custom of bribery.

Although these circumstances explain the reasons for bribery, they do not justify them. The Apostle Paul was held a prisoner in Caesarea for two years by an unscrupulous Roman governor Felix because "he hoped that money would be given him by Paul" (Acts 24:26). Today, nearly two thousand years later, we still benefit from Paul's ethical values which did not permit him to stoop to yielding to this kind of blackmail. If Paul refused to pay a bribe, even when his very life was at stake, the Christian entrepreneur of today should find it exceedingly hard to justify such measures for the sake of economic gain.

I have reviewed some of the ethical problems which are faced by entrepreneurs today who attempt to be faithful to their Christian calling. Some of these ethical problems involve relatively simple decisions of right and wrong. Some of them constitute ethical dilemmas where several alternate courses of action (or inaction) must be assessed for their relative "rightness"—perhaps choosing the least objectionable one. In the next chapter I will turn to some of the still more difficult problems that entrepreneurs face as they seek to determine their standard of living.

CHAPTER 5

A Christian Standard of Living

Chapter two stressed the importance of the use of capital in the productive process. Probably the most important source of business failure is the attempt to engage in a business which does not have adequate capital. It was also pointed out that the source of capital is saving. Savings arise whenever people consume less than they produce. A measure of self-discipline is required for anyone who attempts to save. But saving is vastly more difficult for persons who are currently producing at a level near to bare subsistence. Likewise, it becomes easier to save as one's income level increases.

The standard of living in the United States makes it possible for people at many different income levels to save at least modest amounts. Much of this small-scale saving is channeled to savings accounts in commercial banks, savings and loan associations, credit unions, and other "financial intermediaries" such as mutual funds and life insurance companies. These financial institutions are then able to use the savings they receive to make loans for the purchase of homes (a form of capital), for the purchase of consumer durable goods (another form of capital), and for business loans and other purposes. In 1978 "private domestic deposits" accounted for $131 billion of the total of $394 billion of funds raised in United States credit markets.[1]

Importance of Profits

Many of these "private domestic deposits" are, of course, not just the savings account of the small-scale individual saver but are rather deposits by businesses. But businesses also raise money through the sale of stocks and bonds and above all through a reinvestment of past profits. In the minds of many businessmen this is one of the major justifications of the profit system: profits enable the business to accumulate capital. The accumulation of capital makes the business more productive and thus provides more jobs and enables the business to pay higher wages to the employees. As pointed out in chapter two, this phenomenon is not unique to the "capitalistic" countries of the West. Communist or socialist countries use even stronger methods to accumulate capital. By keeping consumer prices well above the costs of production, the governments of these countries force savings which form the basis of capital accumulation and, hopefully, of rapid economic growth and development.

Profits, therefore, are highly important for capital accumulation. But the problem is that there is no automatic assurance that profits will be used for this purpose. Instead the profits may be used to pay higher dividends to the stockholders or higher salaries to the managers. These higher dividends or salaries may be saved by the stockholders, or they may be spent to increase their standard of living, or they may be given to members of the family, to heirs, or to the work of the church. Herein is the crux of the problem facing Christian entrepreneurs today. How much shall they reinvest in their business? How much shall they spend on themselves and their families? How much shall they give to the work of the church or other charitable causes? In this chapter I want to examine the question of the Christian standard of living. In the next chapter I will discuss the matter of gifts to the church.

Is the Capitalistic System Inherently Unfair?

Some Christians, particularly those in the so-called Third World countries, believe that it is inherently impossible to answer this question fairly under a capitalistic form of economic order. I am referring here especially to the "revolutionary" Christians in some of the Latin American countries today such as Gustavo Gutierrez of Lima, Peru; José Miguez Bonino of Buenos Aires, Argentina; Juan Luis Segundo of Montevideo, Uruguay; and José Porfirio Miranda of Mexico. All of these men have been considerably influenced by Marxism and support certain policies of the current government of Cuba in the Western Hemisphere and China in Asia. While borrowing from Marxist economic analysis they do not advocate all of the Marxist program. In particular they do not want to surrender democratic freedoms. But they believe that the Old Testament prophets and the teachings of Jesus attack the very principle of private property itself. They believe that individual greed is required to make the system of private property work and that this greed is a denial of basic Christian values.[2]

I have much sympathy with this point of view—especially because I think that it stems in part from the incredibly inept way in which the governments of their countries have corrupted the capitalistic system. I am much less sanguine, however, in accepting what I consider to be their naive belief that a change in the political or economic system would solve the problem. If the crux of the problem is greed, as I am inclined to think that it is, I do not concede that the collective greed of a socialist state is inherently better than the total of individual greeds in capitalistic societies.

Furthermore, although large salaries are paid to managers of great corporations in the United States and Canada, salaries and innumerable perquisites have been paid to the managerial class in the Soviet Union. The result is what Milovan Djilas, the Yugoslav communist, called "the new Class . . . those who have special privileges and economic preferences because of the administrative monopoly they hold."[3] A Soviet journalist is reported irreverently to refer to this new class as "our communist nobility."[4] In pure money terms their salaries may be less than the salaries paid to high management personnel in American corporations, but it is the "hidden incomes of the Soviet elite" which place their standard of living far above the rank and file of their fellow countrymen. These hidden incomes take the form of freedom to travel abroad (where they buy for their personal use—or for highly profitable resale—products not available in the Soviet Union), the exclusive use of cost-free luxury cars owned by the government, and luxurious vacation homes (dachas) in the countryside.

These facts are well known, of course, to many Marxists who still favor the system of state communism. But they regard the present system in Russia as a "bourgeois" deviation from the Marxist ideal, and choose as their model what they consider to be a purer form of Marxism in Cuba and the People's Republic of China. Objective reports from these countries would seem to confirm that they have avoided the excesses which currently plague the Soviet Union. Perhaps this greater purity can be maintained indefinitely. But the communist society is only twenty years old in Cuba and thirty years old in China (in contrast to its sixty years of history in Russia), and it seems fair to ask whether as they age they may not assume characteristics which resemble those in Russia. The apparent swing to the right in China following the death of Mao means that incentives will play an increasingly important role in the Chinese economy in the years ahead. Castro is also reported to have said that Cubans will not work without increased wage differentials and incentives. These developments are logical outcomes of the pervasiveness of human greed.

Biblical Versus Marxist Ideals of Property.

The biblical ideal is that all property belongs to God and that man is God's steward in the management of this property. The Marxist ideal is that all property belongs to "the people" but for practical reasons they too must find certain individual persons who will assume stewardship or management functions. The Christian believes that the individual, though born in sin, can be redeemed by the blood of Jesus Christ so that he can enter into a "new creation" (2 Cor. 5:17). Though this does not relieve him from temptation, including the temptation of greed, this new person is now "in Christ." Christ took upon himself our sin in order that he might reconcile us to God. It is this reconciliation which gives us the strength "to lead a life worthy of the calling to which you have been called . . . to mature manhood, to the measure of the stature of the fulness of Christ" (Eph. 4:1, 13). Furthermore, this "new creation" is a part of the church—the body of Christ. This church, formed by Jesus Christ himself, has been given by him the power of discernment—the power to bind or to loose (Mt. 18:18; 16:18, 19).

This is the tremendous, the truly earth shattering, advantage which the Christian entrepreneur has over the manager of a business enterprise in a communist country. They think they live in an "atheistic" state but in fact they operate with a faulty theology. They believe that man is essentially good but that he has been corrupted by a bad economic system. When communism creates a new economic system, man's essential goodness will assert itself. The Christian, on the other hand, can only confess that far from being inherently good, he has an inevitable propensity to sin, but he has the Holy Spirit working in him to free him from this bondage to sin. He needs the help of fellow believers in this—the church—others who likewise have entered into the new creation. The challenge to the Christian is to allow the Holy Spirit and the church to help him overcome even his most perverse tendencies toward greed as he struggles with business decisions and with questions of standard of living and life-style.

The Marxist ideal is "from each according to his ability, to each according to his need." In the operation of such an ideal society, no financial incentives should be needed to induce people to work hard. They will work gladly, to the limit of their ability, for the "good of the cause." In practice, this ideal has proved to be impossible to carry out. Instead, some form of incentive payments are made so that those who are considered to contribute more to the production of goods or the rendering of services are paid more than those who are thought to contribute less. This is sometimes done through salary differentials, sometimes through the payment of piece rates, bonuses, and profit sharing, and sometimes through an elaborate system of fringe benefits and perquisites such as I have already described.

On the basis of detailed studies, Abram Bergson of Harvard has concluded that by the 1950s wage inequalities in the Soviet Union were probably greater than in the capitalistic west.[5] It is possible that some of the reforms in the Soviet Union in the 1960s and 1970s have tended to mitigate this inequality for wage earners, though not for the higher echelons of the managerial class. Inequality in China, where the higher paid workers probably get from three to three and one-half times as much as the lowest paid, is considerably less than in the Soviet Union.[6]

Are Material Incentives Needed?

The Bible speaks much about the perils of wealth and about the necessity of those who have this world's goods sharing their abundance with those less fortunate. Perhaps we could argue that the ability of some early Christians to help others in need implies an accepted differential in the rates of compensation they have received. The only specific biblical references to rates of pay are in two parables of Jesus which were probably intended to have spiritual rather than material application. Thus, in the parable of the talents the five-talented person received a reward of five talents, the two-talented person a reward of two talents, and the one-talented person was severely rebuked for this unfaithful stewardship of the one talent (Mt. 25:14-30). On the other hand, in the parable of the laborers in the vineyard, identical pay was given to different groups of workers who had done very unequal amounts of work (Mt. 20:1-16). Jesus himself was a carpenter (Mk. 6:3) like his father, but the Greek word here actually means that he was a skilled artisan—"a mason, carpenter, cartright, and joiner.... According to Justin Martyr [a church father of the second century] he had 'made yokes and plows.' "[7]

Paul's instructions to the church at Corinth about giving

to the poor did not criticize the prior inequalities which made this possible, and he was silent about the manner in which these inequalities had arisen. His only concern was "that as a matter of equality your abundance at the present time should supply their want, so that their abundance may supply your want, that there may be equality" (2 Cor. 8:14).

Perhaps because the Bible says little or nothing about differences in rates of compensation for people with differing abilities or for people who assume differing degrees of responsibility, Christians of our day have developed their own code of behavior. At the risk of oversimplification, I would suggest that this code may be stated as follows: Everyone should work faithfully, utilizing to the full the abilities and skills with which he has been endowed. A tenth of one's earnings should be given for the work of the church; the other nine tenths may be retained by the individual to use as he deems appropriate—for living expenses for himself and his family, for capital accumulation to expand his business, or as bequests to his heirs at the time of death. In this accepted standard much more emphasis has been placed on the importance of giving the tithe than upon a delineation of what are Christian living expenses for a family (the standard of living) or what may legitimately be passed on to heirs.

I do not believe that this widely accepted code is an adequate one. I will say more in the next chapter about the amount of giving for which a Christian today should feel responsible. Here I want to consider the basis on which the Christian businessman decides what he does with the portion of his income which is not given to the church. The importance of using a part of this for capital accumulation in order that the business may be suitably productive in helping meet the enormous needs of the world's rapidly expanding population has already been emphasized. But how much may a business person legitimately retain for his own and his family's consumption? In other words, what is a Christian standard of living?

Biblical Guidelines for a Standard of Living

When one looks at individual passages of Scripture, it is possible to find support for positions which would range from a "good" standard of living on the one hand, to a low, indeed an ascetic, standard on the other. In interpreting the Bible, therefore, one must look not only at individual passages of Scripture in isolation, but at the overall message which emerges from a consideration of the Bible as a whole.

In the Old Testament it is clear that the children of Israel were expected to enjoy the good things of life. The patriarch Abraham was a person of considerable wealth (Gen. 12:5; 13:6). Moses savored the luxury of Pharaoh's court for a period of forty years. The children of Israel suffered genuine hardship in their wanderings in the wilderness between Egypt and Canaan, but when they got to the Promised Land it was to be "a land flowing with milk and honey" (Deut. 6:3). There they could "go to the place which the Lord your God chooses, and spend the money for whatever you desire, oxen, or sheep, or wine or strong drink, whatever your appetite craves; and you shall eat there before the Lord your God and rejoice, you and your household" (Deut. 14:25, 26).

As indicated in chapter three, the Bible does not teach total abstinence. However, this passage from Deuteronomy has to do with the ritual celebrations of God's goodness in his presence. Other Old Testament passages make it clear that drinking in this context does not refer to general patterns of consumption.

After Israel became an established community their style of living became too profligate and the prophets issued stern warnings against their luxurious habits. Amos was caustic in his criticism of women who lightly demanded that their husbands bring them money for drink when the poor were being oppressed and the needy crushed (Amos 4:1). He inveighed against those who "have built houses of hewn stone" when the poor were being trampled upon (5:11). He pronounced, "Woe to those who lie upon beds of ivory, and stretch themselves upon their couches, and eat lambs from the flock, and calves from the midst of the stall; who sing idle songs to the sound of the harp . . . who drink wine in bowls, and anoint themselves with the finest oils" (6:4-6). The English word "sodomy" refers to revolting sexual sins and stems from the account of the wickedness of the citizens in Sodom (Gen. 19:4-11). But the prophet Ezekiel also condemned the city for its luxurious living, for its "surfeit of food, and prosperous ease" (Ezek. 16:49).

Jesus was not an ascetic like his forerunner John the Baptist. His willingness to eat with publicans and sinners led his enemies to declare, "Behold, a glutton and a drunkard" (Mt. 11:19). This charge resulted from Jesus' compassion for the outcasts and disadvantaged of his day. But certainly his eating and drinking was not a way of life of luxury and ease. Jesus' standard of living is more accurately described by his own words to a would-be follower: "Foxes have holes, and birds of the air have nests; but the Son of man has nowhere to lay his head" (Mt. 8:20). When he sent out the Twelve and later the seventy in evangelistic work, he sent them out in poverty (Lk. 9:3; 10:4). He pronounced woe on the rich that was reminiscent of the Old Testament prophets (Lk. 6:24).

Paul's appeal to the brethren in Rome "to present your bodies as a living sacrifice" is a call to a sacrificial standard of living. This is sharply contrary to all that modern consumerism attempts to teach us. Its enormous expenditures for advertising constantly reminds us of its own perverted notion of the "good life." But Paul adds that Christians are not to be guided by worldly standards of the good life. "Do not be conformed to this world but be transformed by the renewal of your mind, that you may prove what is the will of God, what is good and acceptable and perfect" (Rom. 12:1, 2).

The Christian needs to take these Scripture passages very seriously when trying to follow Christ in formulating a standard of living. To do so will require a resolute confrontation with the rising tide of commercial appeals for luxurious living and a widespread pattern of such living on the part of an increasing number of friends and associates. I am going to be specific in my illustrations of what I mean, even though I recognize that doing so may invite some of my readers to laughter in the mistaken hope that I am trying to be humorous or petty. I believe so strongly about the necessity of the establishment of a Christian standard of life that I am willing to run this risk in the hope that my readers, if they do not agree with the specific illustrations I give, will run a similar risk of devising their own illustrations that will more faithfully portray the Christian standard.

Clothing

"And why are you anxious about clothing? Consider the lilies of the field, how they grow; they neither toil nor spin; yet I tell you, even Solomon in all his glory was not arrayed like one of these. But if God so clothes the grass of the field, which today is alive and tomorrow is thrown into the oven, will he not much more clothe you, O men of little faith?" (Mt. 6:28-30). In the very simple economy of Jesus' day the vast majority of the population spent almost all of their income on the basic necessities of life: food, shelter, and clothing. The income of North Americans today is much higher than it was in Jesus' day, and as a result the pattern of family expenditure has changed. We spend larger sums of money for all of these basic necessities. But the proportionate share spent for each changes. The percentage spent for food declines. The percentage spent for shelter doesn't change very much. But the percentage spent for clothing is higher than it was before. The percentage spent for recreation and for transportation is much higher than in Jesus' day—largely because one big item of the consumer budget—the family car(s)—was not available then.

The same generalizations I have made in comparing expenditure patterns today with those of Jesus' day also apply to a comparison of the poor and the rich of our day. Poor people spend most of their income for food; rich people spend more for food than the poor—but the share of their income which is spent for food declines as the income advances. But, except for the very rich, the percentage of the income spent for clothing expands as income expands.

Conspicuous Consumption

If Christian entrepreneurs are successful in their business, their income will grow. Should they follow the usual norm of spending a higher proportion of this income for clothing? The temptation to do so will be strong. More than seventy-five years ago an American economist, Thorstein Veblen, son of Norwegian immigrant parents, wrote a book which is still a good analysis of the foibles of the rich.[8] He contrasts what he calls "ceremonial behavior" with the consequences of industrial and technological employments. The former is static and traditional. The latter is dynamic. It results in what Veblen calls "conspicuous consumption, conspicuous leisure, and conspicuous waste." The large incomes which our technological society confers upon its members are of little value if they cannot be recognized. The result is that we have developed a number of mechanisms to display our achievements. "Conspicuous consumption" is the most efficient way of displaying our success. Automobiles and housing may be used for this purpose but Veblen thought that expenditures for clothing was the most important indicator of all. Veblen also felt that "emulation" is a powerful human drive. Therefore, when the very rich spend much for clothing, their wealth-displaying activities will be spread quickly through all of society.

Our economy today offers much higher incomes to a much larger group of people than was true seventy-five years ago when Veblen wrote. Conspicuous consumption today is not confined to clothing, automobiles, and housing, but is extended to recreational expenditures, travel, and the possession of countless gadgets. But clothing is still an important illustration of the expenditure of much more money than would be needed to treat our bodies with modesty, to protect them from the elements of rain, snow, and cold, or even to make them attractive.

The powerful force is that of planned obsolescence. Styles of clothing change so rapidly that one who keeps up with the changing fashions will find that his/her clothes do not wear out; they only go out of date. In the past women were often considered to be especially susceptible to the demands of rapidly changing fashions, but in recent years men have proved that they can be equally vain. Thirty years ago the lapels of suit jackets were wide and double-breasted suits were commonly worn; suits with vests were the norm for winter wear. Trousers were pleated in front and were full-cut. A few years later double-breasted suits were considered hopelessly archaic, trousers were "pegged," and vests were virtually unknown. Jacket lapels became narrow. Still more recently lapels have once again widened and suits with vests are sold even for summer wear. Air conditioning, another form of conspicuous consumption Veblen never heard about, makes this tolerable even in the hottest seasons. A few years ago leisure suits were considered appropriate even for business wear. Today, after many men have a good supply of such suits, it is said that such suits are no longer "appropriate." Neckties were once wide, then they were narrow, then they became both wide and long, and now they seem to be narrowing again. Shirts for businessmen were once white, then they became colorful with large figures and wide stripes, now they are more conservative once again.[9]

If a person has only one suit and a couple of ties and shirts it might be possible to wear them out before they go "out of style." But conspicuous consumption requires the well-dressed businessman to have as many suits, shirts, and ties as he can afford—or better still, more than he can afford. The result is that increasingly expensive clothing get only relatively limited wear. Good, but outmoded, clothing can be "given to relief" but certainly this is a very inefficient way of helping the poor at home or abroad. It would be far better if we were to reduce our own expenditures for clothing so that we buy only those items which we really need and can wear out, and use the money saved for cash gifts to missions, the church, or charitable institutions.

Some Christians once felt, and a few still do, that uniformity in clothing is the most effective answer to the temptation to follow slavishly the rapidly changing fashions of worldly society. But in this day, when most men's clothes are mass produced, special clothing of a uniform cut must be hand-tailored and in consequence is unconscionably expensive. But the best witness to the conformity of styles promoted by the clothing industry is not the uniformity of dress among Christian peoples. It would be more effective to buy a limited amount of clothing of good quality and to wear it out, even if this means we will often be wearing styles that are no longer "in." We would save even more if we purchased second-hand clothes which have been sold by persons who have been caught in the rat race of keeping up with the current styles.[10] But following this suggestion has the disadvantage of helping to support the price of outmoded clothing sold by the fashion conscious.

Some congregations have been creatively tackling the challenge of developing a simpler life-style. One of these, the Church of the Redeemer in Houston, Texas, has found many ways of sharing resources with each other, including clothing.[11]

Food

The cost of an adequate, nutritious and tasty diet is not large, even in this time of inflation. Poor people are forced to live on relatively small expenditures for food; unfortunately, however, some poor people have an inadequate knowledge of the principles of nutrition and wastefully spend money for "junk foods." If the cost of a carefully prepared, adequate diet is relatively low, why should people feel it necessary to increase their total expeditures for food as their income rises? The major reasons are that they tend to waste food, to eat larger quantities than are needed to maintain healthy and efficient bodies, to eat richer foods than are consistent with good health, and to eat an increasing proportion of meals away from home.

This is a book on the making of ethical decisions in business rather than on the principles of nutrition and the relationship of diet to health, to cardiac diseases, and to longevity. But most people who have studied these other matters would agree that we tend to eat too much and to eat too rich foods. It was not so much a miracle as an application of good nutritional principles that Daniel and his three friends demonstrated to King Nebuchadnezzar several millennia ago. At the end of a ten-day test when they were "given vegetables to eat and water to drink . . . it was seen that they were better in appearance and fatter in flesh than all the youths who ate the king's rich food" (Dan. 1:12, 15).

Because of higher income levels, and because of an increasingly large participation of women in the labor force, many more people are eating meals in restaurants and fast-food outlets. Early in 1977 it was estimated that Americans would spend about $51 billion dining out in 1977 and that this would represent more than a 12 percent increase over the 1976 level.[12] Although inflation could account for about half of this increase, the other half represented the increasing tendency to eat meals away from home. A later report indicated that the actual increase in expenditures for eating out was greater than had been forecast.[13]

Eating out may, at times be an acceptable form of Christian stewardship. It is more efficient than to pay hired help to prepare food eaten in the home as many of our parents and grandparents once did. But it can also be both a form of conspicious consumption, waste, and overindulgence. The "all you can eat" for $5.95 has probably led many (in the interests of "stewardship") to eat more than was good for them. Either the food was "wasted" or "waisted" as it was lodged in parts of the anatomy already expanded beyond the point of good health.

Dacar Associates, Chicago food consultants, estimated just prior to Easter 1978 that there would be 20 million Americans dining in restaurants on Easter Sunday. They also estimated that these diners would take in 40 billion calories or 11 million pounds of body fat.[14] This would average about 2, 000 calories per person for this one meal. When one recalls that a working man does not need more than about 3,000 calories for a full day, that this was a Sunday when most people were not working, and that the average included the intake of women and children as well as men, it would appear that a considerable amount of overindulgence was involved. The average daily caloric intake for an adequate diet for people in the Far East is only 2,300 calories, and many in lesser developed countries subsist on less than 2,000 calories daily.[15]

The Christian entrepreneur faces special temptations and problems in developing an expenditure pattern for eating meals away from home. The "expense account" is a standard perquisite of business life. It is widely believed that some business can be conducted more successfully in the relaxed atmosphere of an expensive eating establishment than in the administrative office. Some customers expect to be "entertained" before they "sign on the dotted line." Both the sales person and the client are well aware that the expense of the meal is not a personal one but a business one. As a legitimate business expense it is a deduction from gross income in the computation of adjusted gross income for the calculation of income tax liability. Depending on the tax bracket, the government may actually bear half or more of the cost of the meals through forgone taxes. This, too, may encourage lavish expenditures. President Carter suggested to Congress that the "three martini" lunch should no longer be considered a deductible business expense. But the pervasiveness of the practice, strong lobbying efforts by business groups (including the expensive restaurants which benefit from the practice), and perhaps general public apathy stymied President Carter's efforts to change the tax rules.

The ethical principles which the Christian entrepreneur faces in dealing with this practice include at least the following. First, do we operate on the shaky principle that the "end justifies the means"? The end, of course, is the successful conclusion of significant business deals. Some customers won't do business with us if we appear to be "stingy" in our entertainment. Therefore, we must be more profligate than we would personally prefer. A little reflection will quickly reveal that moral quicksands are present here. The end never justifies the means. If we accede to lavish expenditures for food, do we also begin to make lavish expenditures for drink? And if our customers drink, do we in the interests of business comradeship drink with them? It is dangerous to go down this road.

Second, once we have become accustomed to the amenities of lavish eating places when we are on business expense accounts, do we thereby increase our own customary standard of living when eating out for nonbusiness purposes?

And third, "there is no free lunch." Someone must ultimately pay for all expenditures. This may be in part the government through forgone taxes. Other taxpayers must bear the burden of these forgone business taxes, either directly or through the inflationary impact of an unbalanced federal budget. As a business expense it is a "cost of production" and so enters into the price of the goods or service being sold. Like other costs, we will try to pass these costs on to the consumer in the form of higher prices. Do we realize that this is what we are doing? Does our Christian conscience tell us that it is right? I don't think so.

The opportunities for overspending for food are

enormous. For example, it was reported that airline passengers can go to Murray's Sturgeon Shop in Manhattan and spend $45 for a brown bag luncheon ("Airline Survival Package") because their palate is not pleased by the flight meals served by the airline itself.[16] At Palace Restaurant in New York City the average tab for two meals is said to be $225 to $230, but one free-spending couple spent $2,400. The owner, Mr. Frank Valenza, is reported to have disagreed with a New York food critic that the food was magnificent but that "morally the place is an outrage." Valenza was quoted as having responded: "You've made your money, I'm giving you an opportunity to spend it and giving you your money's worth."[17]

At the same time that some enterprising businesses are trying to convince their customers to overindulge, others are trying to help overweight people reduce. One such establishment which charges $900 for a week's regimen of reducing excess body fat, starts its treatment by giving enemas to its patrons. This is followed by a liquid diet and exercises. What a commentary on a civilization built on wasteful indulgence! Jesus once gave a parable of "a rich man, who was clothed in purple and fine linen and who feasted sumptuously every day" (Lk. 16:19). Such people were unusual in the poverty of first-century Palestine. Their life-style is a constant temptation to large numbers among the affluent of our own day.

Expensive Homes

Jeremiah criticized King Jehoiakim for saying, " 'I will build myself a great house with spacious upper rooms,' and [cut] . . . out windows for it, paneling it with cedar, and painting it with vermilion" (Jer. 22:14). What was possible for Jehoiakim by oppressing the poor of his realm is now possible on a much larger scale by the successful businessman of today, even if he pays his workers well. But this does not relieve the businessman of the responsibility of carefully considering Christian stewardship in the construction or purchase of a home. Adequate space is of course needed for a growing family and for providing hospitality for friends and business associates. But since a businessman is more likely to be short on capital in the early years of his career than he is after the business is well established, an anomalous situation often results in which the home is larger after the children have married and left home than it was when they were part of the household.

High building costs and the rapid inflation in land values have resulted in a rapid escalation in the price of homes. To live "near the stars" people pay $150,000 for a cramped two-bedroom cottage in Beverly Hills, California. In fact, such houses are reported to have tripled in price in the past two years. Larger one-family homes sell for up to $4 million each.[18] Homeownership costs have increased more than any other element in the Bureau of Labor Statistics consumer price index in the past ten years.[19] John C. Weicher, Senior Research Associate at the Urban Institute reported that the typical 1976 new home cost $44,200, almost double the 1970 price.[20] By 1979 the Census Bureau reported that the median price of a new, single-family house was $72,000, an eightfold increase in less than 30 years. The average price increased by nearly $10,000 each of the past few years.[21]

Christian entrepreneurs will need to consider carefully whether they are using their home as a way of demonstrating (perhaps unconsciously) their own success. Will they merely go along with the great majority of other people in increasing their expenditures for their homes? Rather, is Christ not calling us to give a counter witness to the prevailing culture by living modestly?

Recreational Expenditures

Throughout much of human history, life was one continuous drudgery of work. Working hard from sunrise to sunset was imperative to provide the bare necessities of life. In ancient Israel these sustained periods of work were punctuated by the weekly Sabbath. All agricultural and commercial activity was forbidden on this day, as were the ordinary household duties. The manservant and the maidservant were to rest on the Sabbath (Deut. 5:14). Those who violated the Sabbath law were to be put to death (Ex. 35:2). While wandering in the wilderness on the trip to the Promised Land, a man was found gathering sticks on the Sabbath. "And all the congregation brought him outside the camp, and stoned him to death . . . as the Lord commanded Moses" (Num. 15:32, 36). The Rabbis even limited the distance one could walk on the Sabbath to what came to be known as "a sabbath day's journey" (Acts 1:12), probably about two thousand cubits or one mile.

In Israel work was interrupted not only by the weekly Sabbath but by several annual festivals. Jesus' family, for example, made it a practice to go "to Jerusalem every year at the feast of the Passover" (Lk. 2:41). This was an eight-day feast (Ex. 34:18). Some of the other annual festivals lasted only one day; others such as the "feast of the booths" lasted seven or eight days (Lev. 23:39-43).

The rigid Sabbatarian laws of the Bible made a profound impact on the Christian community as well. Although Jesus rejected the ridiculous extremes to which Sabbath observance was sometimes carried, his dictum that "the sabbath was made for man" implies that he recognized the values of a rhythm of rest amid the incessant toil dictated by the stern economic realities of the time (Mk. 2:23-28). Through most of the years of the Christian era a day of rest has regularly punctuated a week of unremitting toil. Sabbatarian sumptuary laws of Europe were matched by American puritanical legislation known as "blue laws"—after the blue paper on which they were printed. Although we usually think of these laws today as regulating commercial activities on Sundays, in their Puritan New England origin they also prohibited most forms of recreational activity as well. Secular amusements and all unnecessary work were prohibited; books, plays, and other forms of entertainment were censored.

The complete secularization of American society is probably nowhere more clearly illustrated than in attitudes toward recreation. For years the pattern of labor on the farm and in the early factories was a long working day for six days and a day of rest on Sunday. But by the present century rapid increases in technology made possible shorter working weeks, thereby vastly expanding the opportunities for recreational and leisure activities. By the 1930s the 40-hour week became standard with penalty overtime rates applied when people were asked to work more than the 40-hour week. Businessmen are often not able to share in the shorter working hours given to their employees; in fact, some businessmen feel driven by the demands of competition to work fifty, sixty, or more hours a week. But even so there are times when the demands of the business are less pressing and the businessman can get away for a much needed rest.

But there are two questions which the Christian entrepreneur will want to ask. First, does the pattern of my recreational activities meet the biblical standards of being a time for meditation and worship, or in "getting away" do I tend to forget God as well as my business? Second, are my expenditures for recreational activities in accord with the demands of Christian stewardship?

"Getting away" is in itself a valuable type of recreational experience. We need time to view our work in perspective, and this can be done sometimes more effectively if we are far removed from the community in which we work. Long-range planning may be combined with recreational activity, and this can be accomplished more easily when our day is not constantly interrupted by telephone calls and pressing business problems. While gone from home on such trips it is usually possible to find a church where one can worship on Sunday morning. But if our absences from home become frequent, genuine church life becomes very difficult. Church is more than going to a worship service at 11:00 on Sunday morning. Real church exists only where there is a caring, compassionate community, where there is sharing in intimate primary groups, and where each member assumes some responsibility such as teaching a Sunday school class, engaging in Voluntary Service, or leading a prayer meeting. If the long weekend away from home becomes a regular part of our routine, church life is bound to suffer.

Recreational activity can also be very expensive. Cottages at the lake must be comfortably furnished—thus duplicating items already provided in a primary home. Motorboats are expensive and it is always possible to get new ones which are larger and more powerful. Commuting from the lake to our business is an added expense. It is not surprising that studies of income show that not only the gross amount, but the proportion, of incomes spent for recreation becomes larger as the incomes expand. "Chicago's Ambassador West Hotel offers a 'Terribly Chic' weekend package at $13,315 a person. It includes a five-room presidential suite and a cocktail party for twenty friends, an orchestra, champagne and flowers to fill the sunken bathtub, and a trip to Las Vegas via a private jet for 'six or seven hours of gambling and frolic.' "[22]

No doubt all of the readers of this book will find this kind of extravagance in recreational expenditure to be repulsive. But an eight-day vacation in Hawaii (economy accommodations) costs $1,100 for a couple and this is the kind of vacation which is becoming increasingly common among successful business people. Two-week ski trips to Colorado are also both expensive and no longer a rarity. Dan West, lay leader in the Church of the Brethren who dreamed up the Heifers for Relief project, said, "I cannot eat cake when others in the world do not have bread."[23] Probably we find this standard of living needlessly austere. But we need the Dan Wests to remind us that our lives will be judged by the kinds of stewardship we exercise in all aspects of living. Today it is not only meat and drink and clothing that "the Gentiles seek" (Mt. 6:31-32), but an array of recreational activities, the desire for which may also be insatiable.

Are Christian Entrepreneurs Entitled to a Different Standard of Living?

I have discussed Christian life-styles in general. Sometimes I have made special reference to unique problems faced by business people. But questions remain. Much more could be said. For example, does the fact that the entrepreneur has taken risks and earned a profit thereby justify the "enjoyment" of that extra income in the form of a living standard above that of other members of the church? Do the uncertainties entrepreneurs accept as normal and the longer and often more intense workweek justify greater indulgences in travel, recreational expenditure, and housing than their fellow church members who are, for example, teachers and have a more secure, but less affluent, income and expenditure pattern?

These are important and legitimate questions. They can

be answered with greater understanding by my readers who are members of the business community than I can as an interested outside observer. I have written this book in the hope that business people will be encouraged to consider them prayerfully.

Personally I feel that there are certain ways in which each profession or occupation will have to develop its own life-style. The requirements of clothing for the Christian in business are obviously different from those of the blue-collar worker. But I would add that the Society of Brothers sells a lot of toys, and they don't make adjustments in their clothing as a result of their success in toy manufacturing!

I am not convinced that anything really justifies indulgence. Others work long hours too. Even the 40-hour per week blue-collar worker may feel constrained to "moonlight" and in consequence may work as long a workweek as the entrepreneur. Indeed the constraint may arise in part by a desire to emulate the successful business person. The successful teacher's work is never done. Longer hours of study will pave the way for more effective classroom discussions. Time-consuming scholarly research will fulfill the scholars' sense of obligation to the academic community which has nurtured them. Nor is it clear that the entrepreneurial risk is more onerous than risk inherent in a blue-collar job. The failures of entrepreneurial risk may result in a serious loss of income or even eventual bankruptcy. But the result of this failure may also be the loss of jobs of blue-collar workers who had been working for the entrepreneur. This too means a serious, and perhaps disastrous, loss of income. Depending on the age and qualifications of the worker it may not be possible to find a new job to replace the one which was lost. If a new job is found, it may pay a considerably lesser wage than the one which was lost. The entrepreneur inevitably takes risks, but so do the workers.

In the formulation of ethical standards, it is really not very helpful to say that my problems are different from my brothers and that these differences justify differing standards. There still are absolutes, even if the complexities of twentieth-century life make it more difficult to ascertain precisely what they are. The church has many members. Frank Christian sharing among these members should help us ascertain appropriate Christian ethical standards for all members even to the extent of applying these standards to members of the church with widely differing occupational responsibilities.

How Can We Establish Our Standards?

You may find my discussion of the Christian standard of living in the previous pages to be vague and unsatisfactory. It would have been so much easier if I had said precisely what I thought it should be. Then the reader could either agree or disagree and perhaps go on in much the same way as before. Over and over I have taken the position that the problem of establishing a Christian standard of living is primarily one of finding a suitable pattern for our own lives that lies somewhere along a continuum between utter austerity at the one end and utter profligacy at the other. And, as is usual on a continuum, there are a large number of shades of gray between white and black. But the very difficulty of finding a position which we feel will accord with biblical principles of stewardship does not excuse us from the necessity of establishing it. The task is clearly too great for one or two persons (perhaps husband and wife) to accomplish independently. We need the help of a discerning community. The church should be this discerning community.

We are living in a time of transition in the church. When

the horse and buggy were the only means of transportation, most congregations were relatively small. The congregation was a primary social group as well as a worshiping community. Social interaction after church was very important; often several families joined for the Sunday noon meal. In the afternoon the adults talked and the children played together. "Discernment" was a word which hadn't reached our vocabulary, but in an unstructured and informal way it was going on nonetheless. The Sunday evening "Young People's Meeting" often included opportunities for discussion and further fellowship. Midweek prayer meetings strengthened church life; annual revival meetings renewed it. Church outreach was more than just theory when groups of individuals within the congregation courageously established mission outposts.

In the past twenty years many changes have taken place. Perhaps the most profound is the much wider participation by church members in service clubs and community activities. We do not expect such groups to provide Christian guidance concerning a suitable standard of living. As new group involvements emerge, some of the former ones have disappeared. In many communities the midweek prayer meeting is gone; Sunday evening services where they persist are often poorly attended. We receive instruction in the Sunday morning church service and some genuine discernment often is a part of the Sunday school hour. But are these activities really adequate as a means of helping each other cope with the enormous problems of applying our Christian faith and ideals to the complicated problems facing the businessman? I don't think so.

Special Groups to Help Us Discern God's Will

Two other developments offer promise. The one is the

small group within the congregation often referred to as the "K group," after the Greek word *koinonia* meaning communion, association, or partnership. Applied to church life this has resulted in the formation of groups of eight to twelve members which meet regularly (often weekly) in homes for intimate spiritual communion and participative sharing in a common religious commitment. Social interaction and the sharing of food may be included along with periods of prayer, Bible study, and the discussion of issues relating to living the Christian life. The amount of time spent on these several elements undoubtedly varies widely from group to group, but even in groups which are mainly social, some discernment may well be an informal consequence of the fellowship.

Some church members feel threatened by the presence of these K groups within a congregation. They regard them as fostering cliques and resulting in divisiveness. This fear is not wholly unfounded, but the burden of proof rests upon the critic to suggest more creative alternatives for intimate Christian fellowship.

The other development is interest groups on a denomination-wide basis. Perhaps the earliest of these is the Mennonite Nurses Association which was founded in 1942. The Mennonite Medical Association was founded in 1948 and now has annual meetings which bring together doctors and nurses as they discuss ethical issues in their profession and plan supportive service activities. The Mennonite Graduate Fellowship has met annually since 1958 to provide a forum whereby graduate students can secure counsel from each other in relating their studies to their Christian faith and commitment.

Businessmen were a bit slower to organize. Many informal discussions among small groups of business people were a part of the "Business and Professional Week" at church camps such as Little Eden and Laurelville Mennonite Church Center for the past twenty-five or thirty years. But formal organization on a churchwide basis awaited the formation of Church Industry and Business Associates (CIBA) in 1969 and the Mennonite Business Associates (MBA) in 1973. Three years later these two groups merged into Mennonite Industry and Business Associates (MIBA). The 1978 *Directory* of this organization lists over 7,500 names. Many of these are not members but they are all at least sufficiently interested to have submitted their names. The organization sponsors annual meetings which draw participants from all parts of the United States and Canada, as well as regional meetings. These meetings likewise provide opportunities not only for fellowship and instruction but also for discernment.

Congregational K groups and denomination-wide associations of business people have weaknesses as well as strengths. If the K groups are composed of individuals with similar income levels, they may inadvertently serve as engines for escalating standards of living. If members always support each other in their expanding scales of living, they may remove the salutary influence of "guilt" in restraining a drive toward affluence in life-styles. If K group members never get beyond "praising God for their affluence," they may only be dodging the troublesome question of what really constitutes a Christian life-style. Such consideration is all the more important because of the striking escalation in standards of living in the past twenty or thirty years. We simply must stop to view soberly the question of whether an increased standard of living is what God really intends for us as the result of the amazing growth of productivity in our economy.

Do Different Vocational Groups "Need" Different
Living Standards?

Certainly one of the factors which greatly complicates the discernment of a Christian standard of living is that what seems to be extravagant spending by members of one vocational group, as judged by people outside the group, may appear to be legitimate or even necessary by the "insiders." For example, does the surgeon whose exacting work may mean life or death to his patient have the need for more frequent, and perhaps more costly, recreation and vacations than the office worker who follows an 8 to 5 routine? Does the Christian entrepreneur who frequently faces financial decisions of great consequence affecting the welfare of many workers likewise have the need for costly vacations or recreation similar to that of the surgeon? May a teacher, to assure creative and alive classroom discussions, justifiably spend more for books, magazines, and educational travel than a factory worker? Should a pastor have a larger house to simplify his entertainment of members and visitors? Need a salesman spend more for clothing, for meals away from home, and for entertainment of customers?

It is easier to raise these questions than to answer them. Careful Christian discernment would likely conclude that genuine differences in "needs" exist between vocational groups; this suggests different expenditure patterns in the establishment of a "Christian" standard of living. But to what extent are we meeting "needs" and to what extent are we trying to rationalize the fulfillment of "wants" that go well beyond our "needs"? As a teacher I may buy books and magazines which help me in my teaching. But they may also constitute a form of "conspicuous consumption"—a means of impressing others with my erudition or perhaps even (unconsciously) of my affluence. My office is located in a college

library which has more than 140,000 volumes and subscribes
to more than 725 current periodicals. I must assess my need
for personally owned books and magazines in the light of the
ready availability of this large store of institutional
property.[24]

I think that this is the challenge that faces people in every
walk of life as they seek to determine the pattern of Christian stewardship in the complicated situation we find
ourselves in today. I stated earlier that it is a task that is too
big for each person to decide independently. One needs the
critique of Christian friends who are willing to speak "the
truth in love" (Eph. 4:15). The Apostle Paul gave this
counsel as he recognized the need for unity in a church
where there was a diversity of gifts. He saw clearly that we
cannot be united in Christ's body unless we deal with our
spiritual siblings on the basis of loving candor.

The details of our problems today may differ from those
in Paul's time. But to bring unity to the church today each
member needs the loving critique of fellow members. It is
only then that we can move beyond simplistic "standards"
which do little more than assert that we are "justified" in
spending what we can "afford." We think we can afford to
spend what we earn after having accumulated the capital
needed to expand our business and after we have given our
tithe to the church. But in a growing business the needs for
capital accumulation are well-nigh insatiable. The pressures
of advertising and the unholy desire for conspicuous
consumption combine to make it difficult to give the full
tithe to the church. I am going to suggest in the next chapter
that the 10 percent rule, though probably satisfactory for
low-income groups, is simply not adequate for middle- and
higher-income people.

CHAPTER 6

How Much Shall I
Give to the Church?

In his letter to the Romans Paul discusses the various gifts of the members of the "body of Christ," the church. "Having gifts that differ according to the grace given to us, let us use them: if prophecy, in proportion to our faith; if service, in our serving; he who teaches, in his teaching; he who exhorts, in his exhortation; *he who contributes, in liberality;* he who gives aid, with zeal; he who does acts of mercy, with cheerfulness" (Rom. 12:6-8, emphasis added).

Paul is saying here that giving is not just a chore to meet the demands of church budgets but that it is one of the charismatic characteristics of the member of the body of Christ. In fact, it is sobering to observe that he includes it on an apparent par with teaching and preaching. People have "gifts that differ according to the grace given to us" but there is no suggestion that people with these various gifts form a hierarchy of any kind—that one gift is in any way superior to any other. Instead Paul seems to be suggesting that the ability to contribute financially to the work of the church is an ability some members of the church have in greater measure than others. Those who possess this ability should use it liberally; they should not seek merely to meet a mechanical 10 percent rule.

I have already made it clear that the productive powers of North American businesses permit the attainment of a high standard of living and the accumulation of unprecedented amounts of capital, while still leaving large amounts available for significant gifts to the church. The task of the Christian entrepreneur is to decide the relative share which he will devote to each of the three items I have mentioned. In the last chapter I discussed some principles and problems in determining a Christian standard of living. The amount of one's income which should be devoted to çapital accumulation is related not so much to one's Christian commitment as to the nature of the business and the opportunities for productive investment which it affords. But how much should be given to the church? How much of this should be given now out of current income? How much shall be given later on after the business has expanded and has become more productive? How much shall be willed from the estate at death? These questions are easier to raise than to answer, but the Christian entrepreneur must face them nevertheless.

The Biblical Tithe

For many people the simplest answer is to give a tithe—or 10 percent of one's net income. There are several reasons for this. The most important one is that it seems to have biblical support. "And Abram gave him a tenth of everything" (Gen. 14:20; see also Heb. 7:8). This indicates a very ancient practice of giving a tenth of one's gain to the sanctuary. As more stable agricultural practices developed, the patriarchs continued to give a tenth of their annual produce. In his covenant with the Lord following his dream at Bethel, Jacob vowed that "If God . . . will give me bread to eat and clothing to wear . . . of all that thou givest me I will give the tenth to thee" (Gen. 28:20-22).

In the Mosaic legislation, the law of tithes is given in successive forms. In Deuteronomy (14:20-29) provision is made for the paying of tithes to the sanctuary, to be eaten there by the one giving the offering and by the Levite. But for those who lived a great distance from the sanctuary, the gift might be commuted into money to be spent in a sacrificial banquet. Every third year the tithe was to be distributed to Levites, strangers, and the fatherless. The difference between tithes and firstfruits was not always clearly marked, except that the firstfruits were offered to the priests.

Tithes were prescribed as a means of support for Levites (Num. 18:21 ff.). This seems to have been a remuneration for their services in lieu of a share in the land "for an inheritance." But the Levites themselves were required to give of this tithe to the priests "a tithe of the tithe" (Num. 18:26). Both of these forms were pure land taxes and did not include a tithe from the flock or herd. Therefore a third form of the tithe was required: "the tithe of herds and flocks, every tenth animal" (Lev. 27:32; 2 Chron. 31:5, 6). In later Judaism these forms were combined, yielding two tithes, or an aggregate of one fifth (20 percent) of the product of both soil and cattle.

The tithe was practiced in New Testament times (Lk. 18:12) but Jesus criticized it as being inadequate (Lk. 11:42). Jesus' ideal was the widow with two copper coins who put in the treasury "all the living that she had," not the rich who "contributed out of their abundance" (Lk. 21:1-4). In contrast the Pharisees, with characteristic insistence on the literal observance of the Law, tithed even the smallest of garden herbs (Mt. 23:23).

Most People Don't Tithe

The second reason why many have considered the tithe to be the most effective guide for a suitable amount of giving is a very practical one. If the average person actually gave a tenth they would be giving substantially more than they now do and the total resources available for the work of the church would greatly increase. Commerce Clearing House, a tax information service, examined the United States' income tax returns for 1976 (the most recent year for which figures were available) to determine the amount of charitable contributions and interest payments made by persons who itemized these deductions. They found the following:

Adjusted Annual Gross Income	Contri- butions	Av. %	Interest	Av. %	Fed. Income Tax	Av. %
$10,000 to 15,000	$414	3.3	$1,378	11.0	917	7.3
$15,000 to 20,000	472	2.7	1,690	9.7	1,966	11.3
$20,000 to 25,000	542	2.4	1,836	8.2	3,095	13.8
$25,000 to 30,000	646	2.3	1,977	7.2	4,272	15.5
$30,000 to 50,000	939	2.3	2,366	5.9	7,974	19.9
$50,000 to 100,000	2,015	2.7	3,954	5.3	22,160	29.5

Source: *Wall Street Journal*, Aug. 16, 1978. I have added the two columns on Federal income tax and its percentages of income as provided in the 1976 tax law for a family of four.

This table shows a number of interesting things. In the first place, the average American taxpayer deducts three times as much for interest payments as for gifts to charity. Probably the major reason for the high interest payments is the fact that many people buy their homes, their motor cars, and other consumer durable goods on time payments through the use of borrowed money. Apparently most people consider it more important to own a good home or car than to support the work of the church or to give to charitable causes.

In the second place, the average charitable gift was never more than one third (and at some income levels less than one fourth) of the biblical tithe. Furthermore, although this is not revealed in the statistics, only a part of these small gifts represented gifts to the church. Giving one percent of one's income to the United Fund is considered a "fair share" in many communities and almost obligatory. I do not think that it is an exaggeration to say that contributions to the church or church institutions represented on the average only about one percent of adjusted gross income. Of course the figures given in the table above are for Americans generally, not just church members. One hopes that the figures for church members would be higher. But, as I will mention later, studies of Mennonite giving show that they, as a whole, gave only half of a tithe. If Christian people could only be convinced to give a tenth of their income to the church there would be an enormous increase in the resources available for the work of the church.

In the third place, within the income range indicated by the table, the percentage of the income given as contributions actually decreases as the income increases up to the $50,000 annual income level and increases only slightly above that level. (The Commerce Clearing House figures for incomes above $100,000 are so incomplete as to preclude calculation of percentages. It is probable, however, that if we had the complete figures the percentages would be larger than those for the smaller incomes shown in the table. They show, for example, that at these levels charitable contributions are actually larger than interest payments.) This is in sharp contrast to the percentage going to income tax payments. The Federal income tax structure calls for taxation at "progressive" rates. I will return later to a discussion of the implications of this for Christians who wish to give "as the Lord has prospered" them.

Other sources also indicate that most Americans, in developing their personal budgets, do not consider tithing to be a rule for charitable contributions. One national estimate indicated that charitable contributions were only 1.4 percent of personal spending.[1] The Heller Committee for Research in Social Economics at the University of California surveyed actual living costs for families at two income levels in the San Francisco Bay area. At the lower income level representing wage earners, charitable contributions came to 1.5 percent of the family budget. At the higher level representing salaried persons, contributions were 1.8 percent of family income.[2]

The most striking illustration of how pitifully small charitable contributions may be was provided when President Nixon was in trouble because of the Watergate investigation. The Internal Revenue Service audited his tax returns. They raised questions about his deductions for gifts of some of his personal papers to the National Archives. Actual charitable contributions which President Nixon had made were only a few hundred dollars—less than one tenth of one percent of his income.[3] How many other persons with large incomes give only negligible amounts to charitable causes? A corporation can deduct up to 5 percent of its pre-tax income as gifts to charity or educational institutions. It is reported, however, that on the average most corporations donate only one percent of their pre-tax income to charity.[4]

Many Mennonites Don't Tithe Either

For many years there have been attempts to study the pattern of Mennonite giving. These studies have shown that Mennonites have been much more generous than the national average but that they have probably given only one half of the biblical tithe. Melvin Gingerich, as director of the Mennonite Research Foundation, calculated Mennonite giving to churches and church institutions in 1951 as 3.8 percent of Mennonite income and he reported that this was actually a smaller percentage than the 4 percent estimated for 1947. But he expressed the opinion that giving to "local charities, Red Cross, and other community causes" probably would have added another one percent. Thus the total would have been nearly 5 percent or one half of a tithe.[5] A report issued by the office of the Mennonite Church General Board a generation later indicated that Mennonites in 1977 were still giving about 5 percent of their income.[6]

In the United States, the Internal Revenue Service is very generous in the proportion of one's income which may be deducted for charitable contributions. The present limitation is 20 percent of adjusted gross income to private foundations and 50 percent to public charities. I understand that Canadian law is not as liberal. But it really doesn't matter how generous the law is if we don't give more than a small fraction of what the law permits.

The Bible Teaches Giving

Why should giving of money to the church be an integral part of the life of the Christian entrepreneur? The most obvious answer to this question is that Christian entrepreneurs are members of the church and they will want to support it. In giving to the church they know where their money is going and that the overhead is small. Most of their gifts support needy causes, not a bureaucracy.

But the most important reason Christian entrepreneurs should give is that it is a biblical command. I have already referred to the Old Testament teaching on the giving of the tithe. But the New Testament is full of teaching concerning giving. When Zacchaeus joyfully told Jesus, "Behold, Lord, the half of my goods I give to the poor," Jesus responded with the reassuring "Today salvation has come to this house" (Lk. 19:8, 9). In contrast, when Jesus faced the young man with impeccable personal habits and scrupulous lifelong adherence to the law, Jesus gave the command: "go, sell what you possess and give to the poor". The young man "went away sorrowful; for he had great possessions" (Mt. 19:21, 22). Jesus' ministry of teaching and healing was supported by people like "Joanna, the wife of Chuza, Herod's steward, and Susanna, and many others, who provided for them out of their means" (Lk. 8:3). Jesus obviously believed in giving.

Giving formed a large part of the concern of the Apostle Paul in his ministry in the early church. There must have been genuine suffering among the members of the church at Jerusalem. On his missionary travels Paul visited churches which, though poor by modern standards, had the financial resources to help meet this need. In his second letter to the church at Corinth he commented at some length on this matter. He commended the churches of Macedonia which though in "extreme poverty have overflowed in a wealth of liberality" (2 Cor. 8:2).

In the two chapters which follow these words Paul outlines carefully the principles of Christian giving. The first principle is one of Christian equality: "I do not mean that others should be eased and you burdened, but that as a matter of equality your abundance at the present time should supply their want, so that their abundance may supply your want, that there may be equality" (2 Cor. 8: 13, 14). The second principle is liberality. This word or its equivalent appears at various places in this letter (8:2, 3, 20; 9:6, 11, 13). The third principle is to make the occasion for giving the gift a joyful one: "God loves a cheerful giver" (9:7). The fourth principle is that the giving should not be haphazard but should be systematic. In his first letter to the church at Corinth, Paul instructed the members, "On the first day of every week, each of you is to put something aside and store it up, as he may prosper, so that contributions need not be made when I come" (1 Cor. 16:2).

A "Progressive" Rate of Giving

The fifth principle of giving is that the size of the gift should be in proportion to the ability of the giver to give—or "as he may prosper," to use Paul's words. What does this principle have to say about the percentage of one's income which one should give to the work of the kingdom? Those who favor tithing believe that the giving of a fixed proportion meets this criterion: the person with $20,000 income should give twice as much as the person with $10,000 income, and the person with $100,000 income ten times as much. I doubt if either Paul or Jesus would have agreed with so simple a rule.

I have already observed that Paul was actually talking about "equality" (2 Cor. 8:14); certainly this could not have been realized unless those with much gave a far larger percentage than those with little. Similarly Jesus, in observing the actual contributions by persons to the temple treasury, commended the poor widow for giving "everything she had, her whole living" in contrast to the rich who only gave "out of their abundance" (Mk. 12:41-44). When economists today speak of a tax system which results in the poor paying a higher percentage of their income than the rich they call it a "regressive" system. Jesus clearly was saying that this is not the way the children of God should give in the new kingdom.

The income tax in the United States, Canada, and most other countries has a rate structure which is clearly not "regressive." In fact, it is not even "proportional"; it is "progressive." In the present law in the United States the lowest income which is taxed is taxed at a rate of only 14 percent. As income advances this rate increases to a maximum of 70 percent for taxable incomes over $200,000 (joint return). Because of personal exemptions the actual effective rate of taxation on *total* income (as contrasted to *taxable* income) is even more "progressive"—going from a low of only a fraction of one percent to a high of nearly 70 percent.

The justification for progressive rates of income taxation is that people should support their government in proportion to their "ability to pay." Almost everyone agrees that the "ability to pay" principle is the most defensible one for determining the tax burden. Not everyone would agree that progressive rates are needed to achieve ability to pay; some would feel that proportional taxation would be adequate. Some feel that progressive rates are needed because of the propensity of wealthy taxpayers to find loopholes in the law which reduce the burden of their taxes. In any event, progressive rates of taxation is the usual practice among governments.

Actually, ability to pay is a subjective and nebulous concept. In its place some have argued that the correct principle should be "equality of sacrifice." Many countries have developed tax systems to try to achieve a greater equality in the distribution of wealth and income among all classes of people. This, too, should have a familiar ring for persons conversant with the biblical teachings. Paul called for "equality." He believed so thoroughly in the importance of Christian giving that to symbolize his belief he insisted on taking the gift he had collected in Europe *in person* to the poor Christians in Jerusalem, even though he knew he was risking arrest, imprisonment, and perhaps even death in going to Jerusalem (Acts 21:10-14).

The Graduated Tithe: Progressive Giving

Ronald J. Sider, in a book which disturbed the thinking of many complacent Christians, suggests that Christians adopt the "graduated tithe" for their giving.[7] Some may find the standards he outlines too austere. He recognizes some of the practical difficulties which a family would encounter in deciding on the precise form which their graduated tithe should take. He is aware that inflation is a pressing problem for many families. He suggests procedures a family should use in deciding its own specific schedule of tithe payments. But even if we take a far less radical approach to life-style than Sider takes, the concept of the graduated tithe would still revolutionize the giving of many Christians in business or the professions.

Sider starts with the poverty level of income, adjusts it upward $1,000, and then applies the conventional 10 percent tithe as the giving share at that level of income. As the income advances, he suggests that the graduated tithe rise in brackets of 5 percent with each additional $1,000 of income. When the family reaches the $25,000 income level all earnings above $25,000 would be given to charity. For those who find this too austere, and I would include myself among them, I would suggest two changes. First, I would use as the base for the 10 percent rate the United States Department of Labor's "low" budget. In 1978 this was $11,546 for a family of four. For 1979 the figure would certainly be about 10 percent higher because of inflation. Sider feels that the Christian should absorb inflationary increases as a means of striving toward a simpler life-style. Again, I agree with the goal, but I find the result needlessly austere—especially in times of double-digit inflation. I would also point out that the base figure we select should depend on the cost of living in communities where we reside. When the national fgure was $11,546 as noted above, it cost $19,030 to live in Anchorage, Alaska (the most expensive city), and $10,288 in Austin, Texas (the cheapest city). But costs of living in rural areas are usually less than costs in the cities.

The exact base figure for applying the 10 percent tithe should be determined in the family forum after prayer and after consultation with others in the local congregation. For sake of illustration here I have arbitrarily selected a figure of $12,000. Instead of Sider's 5 percent increases with each additional $1,000 of income, I am suggesting a 3 percent increase. The table on page 152 shows the resulting income and giving scale from the $12,000 base until a marginal rate of 100 percent is reached at income level $42,000.

This table illustrates giving at various income levels. If you want to calculate the amount for your own income level, simply remember that the marginal rate (the rate on the last $1,000 earned) goes up three percent with each $1,000 of income. I have made the calculations for each $1,000 interval between $12,000 and $15,000 and for $3,000 intervals above $15,000. If you were to calculate your tithe at an income of $22,500, you would do so as follows: Start with the tithe at $21,000 which, as the table shows, is $3,450 with a marginal rate of 37%. The tithe on the next $1,000 is at a marginal

Total Income	Percent tithe (marginal rate)		Total graduated tithe	Personal expenditures and saving	Percent of income which is given
$12,000	10%	(of $12,000)	$ 1,200	$10,800	10%
13,000	13%	(of final $1,000)	1,330	11,680	10.2%
14,000	16%	"	1,490	12,510	10.6%
15,000	19%	"	1,680	13,320	11.2%
18,000	28%	"	2,430	15,570	13.5%
21,000	37%	"	3,450	17,550	16.4%
24,000	46%	"	4,740	19,260	19.8%
27,000	55%	"	6,300	20,700	23.3%
30,000	64%	"	8,130	21,870	27.1%
33,000	73%	"	10,230	22,770	31.0%
36,000	82%	"	12,600	23,400	35.0%
39,000	91%	"	15,240	23,760	39.1%
42,000	100%	"	18,150	23,850	43.2%
45,000	100%	"	21,150	23,850	47.0%

rate of 40% (37% plus 3%) for an amount of $400. The tithe on the last $500 is at a marginal rate of 43% (40% plus 3%) for an amount of $215. The total tithe on $22,500, therefore, is $4,065 ($3,450 plus $400 plus $215). These figures are given not to provide a new legalism but to suggest a new pattern which will provide additional joy to the giver. "Each one must do as he has made up his mind, not reluctantly or under compulsion, for God loves a cheerful giver" (2 Cor. 9:7). Those who pay federal income taxes out of their income often resent the amount the government takes, partly because they disapprove of the way the government spends the taxes received. In contrast, the giver of the graduated tithe to the church takes joy in the thought that, as the income expands, more can be given because the giver believes in the good purposes for which the church spends the money.

It is interesting to note that even at an income level of

$45,000, although the marginal rate is by then 100%, the percent of income which is being given is still below the 50 percent which the Internal Revenue Service permits as the maximum deduction for income tax purposes. If you extend this table to higher income levels you will find that the 50 percent maximum is not reached until the $48,000 income level.

If, at high income levels, you make the size of contribution this table suggests, you should be prepared to explain your giving pattern in an Internal Revenue audit. This should not be regarded as an annoying waste of time but as an opportunity to witness to the auditor the joy you have had in being blessed with an income which has enabled you to give in this way.

Except in periods of great emergency, such as total war, national income tax schedules have never reached marginal rates of 100 percent, as is suggested for the graduated tithe. Governments have felt that when marginal rates become 100 percent (or even close to that figure) they become counterproductive. Taxpayers simply make no effort to earn when they know that *all* the additional income they earn will go to the government. Two comments are in order on the contrast between this and the graduated tithe: First, we are living in a time of "great emergency" as Christians; what the government feels is required to "win the war," we as Christians feel is needed to promote the gospel, build up the church, and meet the needs of the world's unfortunate. Second, we do not need the incentives of greater personal expenditure to induce us to earn additional income; our incentive is rather the joy of giving.

Is "Giving" an Unchristian Compromise with the System?
In trying to be faithful to the New Testament ideal, we

must reckon with the fact that two different patterns were used in the early church. The one pattern is the one described in Acts 2 and 4. The members of the Jerusalem church "had all things in common; and they sold their possessions and goods and distributed them to all, as any had need" (Acts 2:44-45). They had achieved equality by changing the economic structure from one of private property to one of common ownership. However, it was a voluntary common ownership. When Ananias, a member of the group, "sold a piece of property . . . and kept back some of the proceeds" Peter asked him, "While it remained unsold, did it not remain your own? And after it was sold, was it not at your disposal?" (Acts 5:1-4). It was a system of free sharing, but not necessarily common ownership of everything.

We do not know how long this system of voluntary Christian common ownership persisted in Jerusalem. The Jerusalem church had to cope with many alien Jewish proselytes who were far from home. It also had to deal with severe famine which stemmed from sources which are not recorded in Acts. "Now in these days when the disciples were increasing in number, the Hellenists murmured against the Hebrews because their widows were neglected in the daily distribution" (Acts 6:1). Perhaps this problem indicates that it did not last very long. This failure of "equality" as reported in Acts 6 could not have occurred very long after the successes reported in chapters 2 and 4. Certainly the New Testament makes it clear that community of goods was not the only pattern in the early church.

The other pattern was one in which offerings were given by those who were blessed with greater abundance in order to share with those who were poor. Most of the Scriptures I have quoted in this chapter represent an application of this second pattern. The Bible does not tell us why Paul tolerated a different pattern from that practiced at Jerusalem. Perhaps the Jerusalem pattern was a viable one only for the local congregation; another pattern was needed for the larger Christian church. Perhaps the Jerusalem pattern did not function effectively after the initial enthusiasm had subsided.

The early Anabaptists were characterized by an intense desire to follow the Scriptures and the example of the early church. "The Hutterite Brethren in Austria and Moravia had adopted the practice of community of goods as early as 1529. They based their economic practices primarily upon teachings and examples from Acts, chaps. 2, 4, and 5 . . . their concept of salvation . . . was not merely personal and subjective, but active and manifested in social relationships."[8] Descendants of the sixteenth-century Hutterite communities migrated to South Dakota from Europe in 1870. They have grown rapidly and have now spread into other American states and Canadian provinces. They still carry on this sixteenth-century Anabaptist practice of communal property. The radical Anabaptists at Münster also practiced community of goods.

However, most of the Swiss and Dutch Anabaptists did not practice community property. "The experience at Münster probably had a negative effect on the Dutch Mennonites . . . Jan van Leiden certainly did not distribute goods in any equalitarian manner as far as his own use of them was concerned . . . the community of goods was associated in the popular mind with the polygamy practiced at Münster. . . . In Menno's 'Reply to False Accusations,' he specifically denied the charge that he and his followers had their property in common. . . . He maintained that the Church was not required to practice complete community of goods even though it was practiced in the New Testament period because the Apostles did not make it a permanent requirement or universal practice." Members of the church should practice "charity and love" and there should not be great "extremes of both riches and poverty. In this way Menno strove to indicate the principle of Christian love in economic practice, without prescribing a specific form for the practice. The terms 'community of production' and 'community of consumption' have been used to distinguish between the practices of the Hutterian Brethren and the Mennonites. The Hutterian Brethren practiced both while the Mennonites only practiced the latter, and that in varying degrees according to the circumstances."[9]

Although Hutterians and Mennonites differed in their practices of property ownership, Menno was especially concerned that there be "no need among us" and that "every need [be] supplied." He felt that the state churches gave evidence of their fallenness by their failure to care adequately for the poor among them. He taught his followers not to make a similar mistake.

"Intentional" Communities Today

The two patterns which existed at the time of the early church are still being practiced by Christians today. To be faithful some Christians feel that they must establish "intentional" communities which seek to replicate for our time the "communalism" of the Jerusalem church. Although they do not actively attempt to change a national economy, they establish an economic order for the local congregation which is radically different from the inequalities which exist in many of the more conventional congregations. Those who believe that "intentional" communities are the only way in which a Christian community can be faithful to Christ will feel that I have not gone far enough in the direction of Christian equality. Instead, they will view what I have written as something of a compromise with the "system."

I addressed this question in the early part of this chapter in my reference to representatives of the "liberation" theology. These people feel that the "power" to determine one's own future is as important as pure economics. They believe that "giving" is not enough if we don't change the structures which are unjust. It is unjust structures which create the ability to give on the one hand and the need to receive on the other. The ability to give arises from inequality, and the giving of excess income only perpetuates this inequality—not only in dollars but also in power and opportunity. The articulate poor do not accept "charity" as a valid Christian relationship. They insist that those aspects of the system which keep them poor must be changed. This means that landholding patterns, the ownership of other resources, and the ownership of businesses must all be changed. Only then can we get beyond charity to the real heart of the issue.

Sharp differences in standards of living within the local congregation can damage Christian fellowship. My suggestions for a graduated tithe would go a long way toward reducing these differences. The establishment of intentional communities of Christians goes even further toward true equality in the Christian brotherhood. (Note that I have not said "achieves true equality." The effective functioning of an intentional community may tend to result in some kind of a hierarchy of political power within the community. Economic equality does not guarantee complete political equality.)

Inequalities between the average standard of living in Christian churches in the affluent areas of North America and Western Europe and the average standard of living in the Third World are the real concern of those who speak of a "liberation" theology. The per capita gross national product in Tanzania is about $160 per year. The per capita income in the United States is more than 40 times as large. As a result of vast national disparities in wealth and income, most intentional Christian communities in the United States still enjoy a standard of living which would seem affluent to a Christian congregation in Tanzania.

Equality of opportunity for Christians all over the world must remain a major goal of Christian action. "Giving" is an important step in reducing the inequality which stands in the way of achieving greater equality. But it must be done with a humility which recognizes it as only an approximation of the Christian ideal. It must never be done as an exercise of power. Jesus criticized those who liked to be "called bene-factors" (Lk. 22:25).

Giving as an Act of Worship

Giving is not only a biblical imperative; it is an act of worship (Rom. 12:1). Worship is a many-faceted experience. It gives honor and glory to God—and this is good because he is holy and everlastingly worthy—but it also enriches the ones who worship. As we worship through song, Scripture, prayer, and the spoken word our spirits are lifted up and the greater the abandonment of our acts of worship the more likely are we to realize a thoroughgoing ecstasy. It is this aspect of worship that gives us the inner resources we need to face with confidence the complexities of life in the world.

In addition to song, Scripture reading, prayer, and preaching the giving of our offering has become a standard part of most worship services. When I was a boy we had a monthly missionary offering and an occasional collection for the modest operating expenses of the local congregation. Our worship has been enriched in recent years by making our giving a regular part of each worship service. A businessman once told me that his most deeply spiritual experience each week occurred each Saturday evening as he sat at his desk and wrote a check for his offering the following morning.

Giving to Meet the Needs of the Church

In the third place, we should give because we want to help meet the needs of the church. What are these needs? They have been reiterated often, but permit me to review them quickly. Giving patterns in the Mennonite Church greatly expanded as a result of World War II. As a witness against participation in the armed forces, the young people of the church declared themselves to be conscientious objectors. The church found it necessary to support these people in Civilian Public Service camps. No longer was a monthly offering adequate to meet a financial obligation of this magnitude. A *weekly* offering became necessary. When the war was over the CPS camps were closed but the church now faced the staggering needs of relief for those who suffered as victims of war's devastation.

The need for relief continues today and will doubtless be a challenge to us for years to come. Now the victims are not only those who suffer from war but those who suffer from natural calamities and from structural inequalities. There are millions of people in the poor countries of the world who have not yet shared in the material benefits of technological advance. To state the need in terms of Mennonite Church institutions, we need not only the worldwide relief program of the Mennonite Central Committee but also the development programs of the same organization. But capital is pitifully short in many poor countries. Mennonite Economic Development Associates (MEDA) is composed of a growing group of business people who share their resources with the poor in this way.[10] The MEDA program should be greatly expanded both in the number of participants and in the amount that each participant will share.

The second general need of the church is in missions—both at home and abroad. The developing mission program at the turn of the century helped the church to start to fulfill a clear command of Jesus. It also gave the church new inner strength by breaking out of the parochialism which had plagued it for more than three centuries. The form which the missionary program took has frequently changed through the years. There is less emphasis on building institutions overseas and more emphasis on developing national leadership. The missionary is not always completely supported by gifts from the home church; Overseas Missions Associates (OMA) support themselves in whole or in part through services they render in the countries where they work. But many missionaries work in programs or in countries where this is not feasible. Substantial financial support is still imperative. Many of our missionaries are serving in countries where price inflation and the fall in the exchange value of the dollar place severe new strains on the missionary budget. These strains have inhibited expansion. In some cases they have necessitated curtailment of programs. In a time of rising affluence, there is no excuse for this.

Local congregational expenses have grown. No longer is it enough to give a few dollars to buy coal for the church stove, paint and repairs for the church building, and Sunday school materials for the children. We have seen that our congregational programs can be enriched if led by a financially supported pastorate. Our Christian education program can be made more adequate if our church buildings have well-designed Christian education facilities. Our youth represent one of our most challenging mission fields. To enter this field we need to make expenditures of time, money, and the construction of physical facilities for a youth ministry.

Christian entrepreneurs will give generously to meet these needs. But they can also render another service which they are uniquely qualified to offer by virtue of their own business experience. As local congregations have moved from simple frame auditoriums to large and complex brick and masonry church plants, the building itself now represents a very substantial investment. The business person well knows that the larger the capital investment, the more important continuous use of the capital equipment becomes. This of course is a major reason highly capitalized business enterprises operate 24 hours a day. They need to do this to get maximum output for each dollar of capital investment. The business person should be able to help the congregation see that it is very uneconomic to have a costly physical plant, most of which is used only two or three hours a week. Christian stewardship requires that multiple-use buildings be the rule.

Other urgent needs demand the gifts of Christian business people. Many activities of the church can be carried out more effectively if organized on a regional or churchwide basis. Mission and relief programs already referred to are clear examples of this. Secondary and higher education programs are another example; large gifts are needed for both capital expenditures and the operating budgets of our schools, colleges, and seminaries. A churchwide Board of Congregational Ministries (Mennonite Church) can provide much needed specialized services for many congregations.

The publication of literature for use in the church, in the home, and for Christian outreach could profit by financial contributions. Because of the large demands for giving by

other church agencies, church publications attempt to
operate on a "pay their own way" basis. Although it may appear to be a sound philosophy to use the market mechanism
to answer the question of "what shall be published?" we
may not be fulfilling our Christian mission if we apply
market principles too strictly. Some books and papers should
be published even if it is unlikely that they will generate sufficient sales to cover production costs. Some books and
papers should be sold below cost in order to meet missionary
objectives in the widest possible market. The "Choice
Books" program of the Mennonite Board of Missions is an
example of this. Finally, a churchwide General Board can be
invaluable in coordinating and promoting the work of the
various institutions and boards of the church and in arrang-
ing churchwide meetings of fellowship, celebration, and discernment.

Perhaps it was a mistake for me to list all of these opportunities for giving in the church today. Often we hear an
opinion expressed calling into question the constant repeti-
tion of requests for funds. But when careful compilations of
statistics of giving indicate that on the average we are giving
only 5 percent of our income, do we really have evidence
that we are being hurt by our giving? Of course averages
conceal wide individual variations. Some members undoubtedly give 10-20 percent or more. Statistics for Mennonite giving may seriously underestimate the giving to
popular evangelical causes such as national TV ministries.

The teachings of Jesus on giving clearly show that the real
measure of our giving is not how much we give, but how
much we hold back for ourselves. As our incomes advance
we tend to hold back for ourselves money which will meet
progressively less-urgent real needs. Our problem is not that
the demands of the church for our gifts have increased but

that our own conception of what constitutes an acceptable standard of living has expanded even more rapidly.

Special Problems Christian Entrepreneurs Face in Giving

Christian entrepreneurs encounter special problems in deciding the appropriate amount in giving to the church— problems which other members of the Christian community either do not meet at all or face to a much lesser degree.

The first of these is the question of whether it is better to give now or to reinvest one's income with a view to giving larger gifts in the future. Previously in this book I have discussed the great importance of capital in modern business. It would not be responsible Christian stewardship to jeopardize future growth (and the possibility of large future gifts) by making current gifts that are unwisely large. At the same time, there is a leanness of soul that comes from a failure to give each week as an act of worship. Capital accumulation in a business is also inhibited by government demands for its tax share of our income dollar. We can't tell the government: "Forget trying to collect taxes from me now, wait until my business grows and you will get a lot more taxes later." We shouldn't try to tell the church essentially the same thing. Perhaps a rule of thumb for a growing business would be to give a tenth. But this would be only a temporary and transitional expedient. If the business prospers, much more than a tenth should be given later.

A closely related question is whether gifts should be made only out of income or whether there are some circumstances where gifts should be made out of capital as well. Some businesses are characterized by relatively low annual income but by substantial capital gains. Farming is an outstanding example of this. The prices of farm products have fluctuated sharply from year to year but within the past decade they

have not gone up as much as the price of the things the
farmer must buy—the farmer's costs of production. Net income, therefore, is low in some years. But at the same time
the value of farm lands has grown. These (usually un-
realized) capital gains are much larger than income from
operations. Should a portion of these capital gains be given?
To the extent that they are paper gains rather than realized
gains, it may seem inappropriate to do so. To sell off a part
of the farm to have ready cash for gifts to the church would
seem to militate against efficient farm management. Yet,
sometime the farm will be sold or passed on to heirs and
gains will be taxed. Is it certain that the best solution is to
wait until that time and then make a large lump sum gift to
the church? If this were done the joy of weekly giving would
be lost and the very magnitude of the "one big final gift"
may cause it to be difficult to make. Regular giving is so important that it should take place even if the giving must be
out of capital.

A third problem relates especially to a closely held,
family-owned business. Operators of such businesses quite
naturally hope that the business will continue after the
original owners retire or die. In many cases there will be an
opportunity to sell the business to a larger firm. This is a
simple solution, and it will be a lucrative one if the larger
firm offers considerably more than the present book value of
the assets. But some business people who have lived to see
the longer term results of such a sale, have come to regret it.
The headquarters of the larger firm are often located in a
distant city (or on occasion even in a foreign country) and
the new top management may not have the same kind of
interest in local projects that the family owners had. It would
be more appropriate to distribute part of the stock to the
workers through employee stock ownership plans (ESOP)

and to give part to church institutions. Although this will dilute the percentage of ownership by the management (family members), it will not likely result in a surrender of control. I will discuss these matters in more detail in the next chapter.

A fourth problem is the extent to which a gift should be a conditional gift. Most church institutions greatly prefer to receive unconditional gifts. They will then use the gifts for purposes which their boards of control think are most urgent or have the longest term significance. These boards are appointed by the church and are designed to be representative of the wider church. But boards are composed of human beings and they are subject to many influences. The verbally articulate may be highly persuasive. If such persons influence church decisions through their verbal gifts of persuasion, business people whose talents are financial may feel that it is not inappropriate to let their money "speak." Thus they may help determine the direction a church or a church institution may go in its program by making designated gifts for certain specific purposes.

There are many differences in the degree of influence which the donor may make through his gift. For example, a donor may specify that his gift to a college should be used to support only one department of the college, e.g., the Bible department. Since a church-related college would have a Bible department in any event, the college may gladly accept the gift, use it for the designated purpose, but use undesignated funds which it had previously used to support the Bible department to finance other aspects of the college's program. The donor has the satisfaction of knowing that his gift has supported a part of the educational program in which he has a deep personal interest. The college, however, can continue to spend the same relative amount of its budget on the Bible department as it had spent before the gift was received.

The donor would have had a greater control over the institutional program if instead of simply designating the gift for the Bible department he designated it for the purpose of *expanding* the Bible department. A college in accepting such a gift would not be free to transfer previously undesignated funds from the Bible to other departments. Donors could exercise even greater control if they would make a gift to the Bible department provided, for example, all faculty members in the department personally subscribe to the dispensationalism of the Scofield Reference Bible. Most colleges would not agree to accept gifts with such rigidly prescribed conditions.

Church institutions would naturally prefer that all gifts be made without any conditions or strings attached. On the other hand, the donor has a right to feel a sense of personal involvement with the gift. The donor, in consultation with the representatives of the institution receiving the gift, should be able to plan gifts which will give at least a gentle nudge to the direction of institutional policy and yet will not, a generation or more later, appear to have been shortsighted or unduly restrictive. Many colleges established a century or more ago, for example, are embarrassed to have endowments for scholarships which are so restrictive that they cannot now find students who qualify for them.

A particularly appropriate way a donor can influence the direction an institution will go is to make a matching gift. Here the gift is made on the condition that the institution raises an equivalent amount of money from other sources equal to the size of the gift. The donor then has the satisfaction of knowing that his gift will not only meet a significant need but will stimulate others to give as well.

Passing Our Estate on to Our Children

In this book I have taken the position that it is incumbent upon the Christian entrepreneur to exercise with great care the stewardship responsibilities which his Christian calling imposes upon him. Honest profits which accrue to the well-run business are to be welcomed, not despised or treated with suspicion, if the business follows Christian practices in purchasing, employee relationships, and sales promotion. Some of these profits may very legitimately be plowed back into the business to expand its operations, to provide employment for additional people, and to make or sell useful products or services. This chapter, on the other hand, has stressed the opportunities for giving to the work of the church and its institutions. Does this provide an adequate incentive for the businessman to produce to the limit of his ability? Or are other incentives also necessary?

For many, passing a substantial estate on to one's heirs at death is a powerful incentive. Some feel that this accords with Paul's warning to Timothy: "If any one does not provide for his relatives, and especially for his own family, he has disowned the faith and is worse than an unbeliever" (1 Tim. 5:8). Others defend it on the pragmatic grounds that this will enable a family business to be carried on intact. Both of these are legitimate concerns, but neither excludes the possibility of giving large gifts to the church. There are other ways in which a family business may be carried on after the one who has founded it and nurtured it has passed on in death. And the actual "needs" of one's close relatives which the Apostle Paul had in mind can hardly justify passing on a large estate. Usually the children are already well-established financially when the parents die. The children can hardly be said to be in "need" of a large estate.

The advice which one very wealthy man, Andrew Car-

negie, gave in his *Gospel of Wealth* is still very much to the
point. He reviewed various ways in which a rich man might
dispose of his wealth. "It can be left to the families of the
decedents . . . [but this] is the most injudicious . . . it is not
well for the children that they be so burdened . . . great
sums bequeathed often work more for the injury than for the
good of the recipients. . . . The parent who leaves his son
enormous wealth generally deadens the talents and energies
of the son and tempts him to lead a less useful and worthy
life than he otherwise would." He applauded estate taxes:
"Of all forms of taxation, this seems the wisest." Carnegie
went on to say that it is the duty of a wealthy man to live
unostentatiously, "to provide moderately for the legitimate
wants of those dependent upon him, and, after doing so, to
consider all surplus revenues which come to him simply as
trust funds . . . to administer in the manner . . . best calculated to produce the most beneficial results for the community."[11]

Does the Christian Entrepreneur Need Material Incentives?

One of the most commonly heard justifications for capitalism is that man is an economic animal and that he will
perform most efficiently if provided with material incentives. Socialist economics has criticized the use of material
incentives and has offered in its place the socialist ideal of
"from each according to his ability, to each according to his
need." But in actual practice this ideal has seldom been
realized. One study which has observed the socialist
economies of Eastern Europe has rejected the opinion that
the pursuit of the socialist ideal has resulted in the greater ef-
ficiency of socialist economies. Although very rapid growth
has occurred in some countries, the gains have not always
been permanent. Overall the socialist economies have

proved to be relatively less efficient than capitalist economies.[12] As applied to farming, "collective farming countries, taken as a whole, have a net product that is still below its prewar level. The comparison with Western Europe ... confirms the impression that socialist farming methods are particularly costly in terms of intermediate consumption."[13]

In the Peoples Republic of China the emphasis on equality has been even stronger than in the socialist countries of Eastern Europe. Economist Kenneth Boulding has expressed the opinion that this may have been necessary because of the very low aggregate gross national product of China.[14] Economist John G. Gurley of Stanford University, one of China's most enthusiastic supporters in the academic community, writes, "The Maoists argue that the pursuit of money as a prime goal of life corrupts the soul. It leads to individualistic, selfish, grasping behavior.... They are, in fact, just the opposite of the traits sought by the Maoists: selflessness, serving the people, honesty.... For the Maoist, the task ... is ... to 'prepare both the material and spiritual conditions for the future communist society.' "[15]

These words read strikingly similar to Christian ideals as expressed in the New Testament. But Gurley admits that the harsh realities of operating a socialist state in China have necessitated some retreat from these high ideals. He says that the goal of "income payments according to need" was "deemphasized" in the early 1960s because of its tendency "to reduce seriously the peasants' work incentives." Private plots where the peasants were free to work as hard as they wanted to work and to do what they wanted to do with the product of their labor were at first condemned as being capitalistic. Later, as a practical necessity, the private plots were restored.[16]

The Christian Vocation of Being an Entrepreneur

Will the Christian entrepreneur be able to operate with a minimum of material incentives? This book has been written in the conviction that this is not only possible but that it is a natural result of the Christian regarding the responsibilities in business as being an outgrowth of the primary calling to be a Christian.[17]

The English word "vocation" comes from a Latin word meaning "to call." We use the word to speak of the vocation of teacher, doctor, lawyer, social worker, merchant, laborer, and many others. But the New Testament makes it clear that these things, though good and useful, are secondary. God "saved us and called us with a holy calling" (2 Tim. 1:9). Members of the church are "called to be saints" (1 Cor. 1:2). Christ, through the Holy Spirit, called us through the gospel (2 Thess. 2:14). "In everything God works for good with those who love him, who are called according to his purpose.... And those whom he called he also justified; and those whom he justified he also glorified" (Rom. 8:28-30). These and many other passages of the New Testament are not written only for "ministers" or for "full time church workers." They are written to churches and are intended for *all* members of the church. In a sense all Christians are ministers—but God has ordained that we minister (serve) in different ways.

This book has been written especially for those who, as Christians, serve God through their daily work in business. We would think it very queer (and perhaps even immoral) if a pastor should tell his congregation that if they pay him $10,000 a year he will do so much work but that if they pay him $20,000 he will be willing to work twice as hard. In other words, we expect that his incentive will not be the material one (size of his salary); it will rather be the inner joy of knowing that he is spending his time and efforts in doing the work his personal gifts and his studies have best qualified him to do.

It is not too much to expect that Christian entrepreneurs will treat their daily work with the same kind of attitudes we expect of the pastor of a congregation. Christian entrepreneurs also have certain personal gifts—gifts which differ in kind from those possessed by our pastors. But by the grace of God these special gifts of the Christian entrepreneur need not be less "spiritual" than those of the pastor or any other member of the church, Christ's body. The physical body has many members, each with different functions, and when each of these parts of the body is healthy the body as a whole is in health. Likewise the church has many members. The church is healthy when each of these members functions as God intended.

We should pay our pastors adequately to meet their needs and those of their families who depend upon them. Likewise Christian entrepreneurs should have income adequate to meet their and their family's needs. But to say that they need much more than that as an incentive to work hard is no more reasonable than to expect a pastor to double his "output" if his salary is doubled. This kind of reasoning may appear strikingly similar to the Maoist China ideals of self-lessness, honesty, and serving the people. As noted, Maoist China had to deviate from these high ideals and introduce greater material incentives to appeal to selfish human instincts. The Christian, however, has resources of God's grace which cannot be claimed by the Chinese or anyone else who rejects the saving work of Christ. It is these higher Christian resources which make the impossible possible. "Not that I have already obtained this or am already perfect; but I press on to make it my own, because Christ Jesus has made me his own. Brethren, I do not consider that I have made it my own; but ... I press on toward the goal for the prize of the upward call of God in Christ Jesus" (Phil. 3:12-14).

In the preface of this book I pointed out that some of my Christian friends may find that the position that I have taken in this book is not a radical one and is, therefore, not completely Christian. Not surprisingly, I do not agree. I think my position is both radical and Christian. To be sure, I do not reject the private ownership of productive capital nor of durable consumer goods. I do not reject the profit system. Instead, I believe that these features of capitalism must be brought under the judgment of Christ so that they serve Christ's purposes in promoting his kingdom in the world. This means that profits must not merely serve the selfish interests of the entrepreneur and his family, which is the usual human tendency.

It requires a leap of faith to believe that Christ's love can transform men and women from selfish, egocentric individuals to loving persons whose interests are rooted in the Christian community and are extended from there to the ends of the earth. But I probably need not remind my friends that it also requires a leap of faith to believe that a viable option is the communal possession of property and a selfless disposition of the fruits of their labor in accordance with the needs of the community. I need not remind them of this because if they have already tried it for an extended period of time they already know that what I am saying is true. They also know that it is possible only through the grace of God as he ministers to them through the work of the Holy Spirit in their individual lives and in their Christian communities. I affirm these friends in taking this leap of faith, unless they accompany it with what I think is a misguided belief that their way is the *only* Christian way.

I believe that the alternative presented by this book is just as Christian, just as demanding. A radical commitment to the use of the fruits of one's labor or of one's entrepreneurial expertise for God's purposes in the world can be just as profound a form of Christian nonconformity as the intentional community. To attain this level of commitment requires resources that go far beyond those of the individual acting alone. Rather, the individual must be willing to be disciplined and counseled by the loving Christian community and, above all, must be submissive to the leadership of the Holy Spirit.

CHAPTER 7

Creative Christian Alternative Forms of Business

Throughout this book I have assumed that most Christian entrepreneurs would operate relatively small-scale businesses. But when business is successful, it tends to grow. As it grows it becomes more complex and both the economic and the ethical problems become more troublesome. As the founders of the business become older they may want to pass the business on to their children or they may sell it to a large enterprise which is seeking to become still larger. Both of these "solutions" present their own problems. The children may not be interested in operating the business, or they may not be capable of doing so. The large impersonal conglomerate may have no interest in carrying on the Christian goals and objectives which the founders deemed important.

There are also important tax considerations. This is not the place to discuss the intricacies of this matter in detail. But if the estate is valued at more than $150,000, a

substantial share of the estate will go to the federal government as estate tax. Provision must be made for the continued
operation of the business and for the payment of necessary
taxes.

The Scott Bader Commonwealth

Some owners have embarked on creative new ways to
view ownership—ways which will solve the problems I have
mentioned above and will make the enterprise more productive as well. The Scott Bader Commonwealth in England is
an interesting example of this.[1] Ernest Bader was a Swiss
Quaker who came to England as a penniless immigrant
before World War I. He established a plastics company in
1920. By 1951 he had weathered the problems of World
War II and his enterprise had grown to a medium scale establishment employing 161 people. It became "a leading
producer of polyester resins and also manufactured other sophisticated products, such as alkyds, polymers, and plas-
ticisers." At that time his sales were approaching $2 million a
year and his net profits were nearly 12 percent of sales. Then
"he suddenly woke up and said, I am now doing to all these
people (my employees) what I suffered from when it was
done to me. I am not going to go out of this life with this
feeling. No, I must do something ... I want to put this on
the basis that I as a Quaker and a pacifist believe in ... I
don't want to have ownership of this company."[2]

Bader felt that he needed to make some decisive changes.
Employee stock ownership (profit sharing) "which he had
practiced from the very start, was not enough." Instead, he
now established the Scott Bader Commonwealth. Ninety
percent of his stock was vested in his organization in 1951
and the remaining 10 percent was turned over to it in 1963.
There are no longer any private owners. The members of the

Commonwealth are the workers, but they are only members as long as they work there. "There are no owners and employees; we are all co-owners and co-employees." As partners, "they cannot be dismissed by their co-partners for any reason other than gross personal misconduct. They can, of course, leave voluntarily at any time." They have imposed upon themselves a number of "self-denying ordinances."

First, "being of Quaker origin, we will not knowingly sell any of our products if we have reason to believe it will be used for armaments."

Second, "the sovereign body [is] a sort of parliament of workers . . . not the board of directors. And they can, in fact, choose or dismiss directors, and have to approve the salaries of chairman and directors . . . there's a high degree of democracy . . . there are constitutional provisions for real participation in decision making."

Third, there is a "maximum spread between the highest paid and the lowest paid of . . . one to seven. There is no pressure from the community that it should be narrowed, because it is understood that this spread is necessary."

Fourth, "we are determined not to grow beyond the size of four hundred." Instead of increasing the size of the original establishment they "have split and put into being three new companies, totally independent." They consider this necessary "to keep the human touch."

Fifth, "when there are profits—and there have always been profits—some money must be put aside for taxation and reinvestment." Sixty percent of the profits are designated for this purpose. The other 40 percent are divided equally between "bonuses to those working within the operating company and . . . to charitable purposes outside."

In the twenty years between 1951 and 1971, sales increased by eight times, net profits by more than four times.[3] Creative uses for the charitable contributions have resulted. But they have also developed projects which are designed to relieve the boredom of the workers by creative leisure activities: a community motorcycle repair shop and a gardening machine pool.

The Scott Bader Company has not been more successful financially than many other companies. "Its merit lies precisely in the attainment of objectives which lie outside the commercial standards, of *human* objectives which are generally assigned a second place or altogether neglected by ordinary commercial practice." Private ownership has become extinct. "No one has acquired any property." On the other hand, "Mr. Bader and his family have ... deprived themselves of their property. They have voluntarily abandoned the chance of becoming inordinately rich.... Excessive wealth, like power, tends to corrupt.... They corrupt themselves by practicing greed, and they corrupt the rest of society by provoking envy.... Mr. Bader ... thus made it possible to build a real *community*."[4]

This has accomplished two important additional results. First, "it has enabled everyone connected with Scott Bader to learn and practice many things which go far beyond the task of making a living, of earning a salary, of helping a business to make a profit.... Within the Scott Bader organization, everybody has the opportunity of raising himself to a higher level of humanity, not by pursuing, privately and individualistically, certain aims of self-transcendence ... but by, as it were, freely and cheerfully gearing in with the aims of the organization itself."

Second, the "one-half of the appropriated profits ... devoted to charitable purposes outside the organization has not only helped to further many causes which capitalist society tends to neglect—in work with the young, the old, the handicapped, and the forgotten people—it has also served to give Commonwealth members a social consciousness and awareness rarely found in any business organization of the conventional kind." As a result the Commonwealth has not "become an organization in which individual selfishness is transformed into group selfishness."[5] In other words it has not fallen into the error I noted in chapter five where I criticized the socialistic societies for replacing individual greed with collective greed.

Bewley's of Dublin, Ireland

Bewley's Cafes Limited is a similar venture but operated on a smaller scale. The leadership of this firm is in the hands of a Quaker family. In the early 1840s the Bewleys opened a shop in Dublin to sell tea, sugar, coffee, and Oriental vases and ornaments. Later a cafe and bakery were developed to sell rolls with the coffee. By 1903 they imported Jersey cattle to provide milk and cream to be sold in the cafe; in 1916 they opened a confectionery shop. The business has continued to grow. By 1978 their sales were approximately $6 million and they had 400 employees. The founder, Ernest Bewley, died in 1932 but his children and grandchildren have carried it on.

"In order to provide a means by which those working in the firm could participate more fully in the company's activities, it was decided in 1971 to form the Council. This body consists of the head of every department, and an elected representative from every department. The Council meets about once a month and discusses various matters relevant to the running of the business.

"The firm started as a very small, privately owned concern. Over the years the value of the capital has grown considerably." By 1978 their assets were valued at approximately $4 million. "All those who have worked in the firm, in whatever capacity during these years have contributed towards the growth in the capital. In 1972 it was decided that the capital should no longer remain in private hands but should be held in trust for all working in the firm both at the present time and in the future. The shares were therefore transferred to . . . '*The Bewley Community LTD*.'

"Any member of the staff who has been with the firm for not less than three years may apply to become a member of the Community." Members are "entitled to vote if it were proposed to sell or wind up the firm or to make changes in the Memorandum and Articles of Association.

"The members of the Community, who are the owners of the shares, can never gain personally from them. No one can ever be tempted to sell the firm for private gain. . . . Any income which the Community may have must be used for specified social objects such as the relief of deprived people, and 'in particular to promote and support efforts to provide employment for such people.' [We seek] to give practical expression to the aim mentioned in the Articles of the Company, i.e., 'To encourage thinking in terms of the welfare of the community in which we live, rather than a desire for personal gain at the cost of others.'

"A profit-sharing scheme has been introduced. A minimum of 60% of the profit must be retained in the company. A maximum of 20% may be paid in bonus to the staff and an equal amount . . . must be paid in dividend to the Community." Those who are on pensions from the company as well as the current employees share in the bonus. The "dividend to the Community" is then distributed to a wide variety of charities. Many of the gifts have been made to organizations which are working for ameliorating the strife which has characterized the Irish scene in recent years. An example of this is their gift to the Glencree Centre for Reconciliation. Other gifts have included such a wide variety of organizations as a Methodist Social Aid Centre, a Catholic Boys Home, a Centre for Alcoholism, etc.

"Many of the evils which threaten the world arise from a 'desire for personal gain at the cost of others.' " The Bewleys have thus changed the structure of their company. They have done so to distribute their wealth throughout the world and to make a positive "contribution towards a better world."[6]

John S. Lewis Partnership, London

John S. Lewis Partnership differs from Bewley's in two ways: (1) it is a much larger business and (2) most of the profits which have not been used for the expansion of the business have been paid to the (presently) 23,500 workers in the form of profit sharing in proportion to the workers' regular pay.

John Lewis began as a small dry goods store in Oxford Street in London in 1864. In the 115 years since then it has grown to one of the largest chain of stores in Great Britain. The chain now includes 17 large department stores and 67 Waitrose supermarkets dealing primarily in food. These stores are spread from Edinburgh in Scotland to the south coast of England. The Lewis chain also engages in some wholesaling and export trade, manufacturing, farming, and fruit growing. Its annual sales have more than quadrupled in the past 10 years and in 1977-78 were valued at £437 million. (Since the British pound is presently worth more than $2, this means that annual sales are nearly at the $1 billion level.) From the beginning the business was characterized by business ethics which were scrupulously honest, by seeking customers through providing a wide variety of merchandise at low prices rather than through advertising, and by developing a reputation for value and fair dealing.

The impetus to provide for profit sharing began in the early 1900s when Spedan Lewis, son of the founder, looked at their financial statement and realized that "he, his father, and brother were jointly drawing from the business . . . substantially more than the whole" payroll for the employees. "From that moment he began his persistent and lifelong effort to devise a more equitable division of the rewards of industry." By 1920 each worker was receiving in profit sharing bonuses an amount equal to 13½ percent of regular pay.

In 1928 John Lewis, the founder of the business, died. Inasmuch as Spedan Lewis' brother, Oswald, had withdrawn from the firm in 1925, Spedan Lewis was now the sole owner. The following year "he made an irrevocable settlement in trust for the benefit of the workers . . . [in effect] he sold to those workers, present and future, the whole of his rights in the businesses." The workers have become the Partnership. The Partnership paid approximately £1 million for Spedan Lewis' ownership rights, an amount "no more than . . . he could very easily get [in] immediate cash in the open market. The members of the Partnership were not to pay any interest on this loan, and were able to spread the repayments over many years."[7]

The productivity of "Partners has been increasing steadily . . . and this has meant that profits have been good. A great part of these profits has been ploughed back into the business" and certainly this steady increase in capital investment has contributed greatly to the high profits. But even after this reinvestment of earnings there have been substantial amounts remaining for other purposes deemed important by the Partnership. "From 1928 to 1970" the workers (Partners) were paid a bonus "in the form of stock bearing a fixed rate of interest (usually 5%)" which the workers were free to sell, if they wished, on the London Stock Exchange. From 1965 to 1970 the bonus was paid partly in stock and partly in cash. Since 1970 the distribution "has been wholly in cash." The bonus is a percentage of the workers' total pay. Since 1966 it has varied from a low of 11 percent (in 1970) to a high of 18 percent in four of the years. The average has been nearly 15 percent.[8]

A part of the profits not ploughed back in the business or distributed as bonuses is used to provide leisure-time benefits for the workers. The Partnership Council has elected a Committee for Leisure Activities. These activities have ranged from "darts to ocean cruising and from tennis to opera." They have provided "a holiday camp and three first-class country clubs" and they have "secured a long lease of the castle and fifteen acres of Brownsea Island in Poole harbour as a holiday hotel." Behind the store "in Oxford Street is a small theatre that is available to the music, operatic, dramatic and film societies" of the workers. "The chess club is one of the oldest of Partnership Institutions and garden society is currently the biggest."

Sick pay is provided up to six months in any year, depending on the length of service, and a claims committee may extend the sick pay beyond this if they deem it necessary. A noncontributory "pension scheme was started in 1941 . . . . This fund has now (1978) accumulated over £40 million." Workers who wish to accumulate a larger pension may voluntarily make additional contributions to the fund, and when they do so the Partnership itself also makes additional contributions. Workers who have dependents and who have been working for the Lewis firm for more than three years are provided a life insurance policy on a noncontributory basis. The death benefit is "a sum equal to two years' pay." Workers receive discounts for purchases in the department stores of 10 percent for the first three years they have worked for the firm and 20 percent thereafter. Workers receive discounts of 5 percent for purchases of food in the supermarkets during the first three years and 10 percent thereafter.

Workers are free to join labor unions and in some sections of the business (notably trucking) "a considerable proportion of Partners are members of a trade union." In these cases "the Partnership provides full facilities for normal trade union consultative machinery if the Partners concerned so wish. In general this operates as complementary to the work of the Partnership's own consultative system." But workers have other avenues for making their wants known. Each of the 26 branches publishes its own local journal called *Chronicles*, usually a weekly publication. The "central editorial department produces a *Gazette* which has an average weekly sale of 14,000 copies." Any worker "can write to the *Gazette* or to *Chronicles* about anything and they can sign their letters or not, as they please."

"Partners mostly trust each others' intentions and goodwill, . . . they are happy and satisfied in being part of a large, successful and famous team and . . . they take pride in high standards of shopkeeping." Although this quotation (as well as others relating to the Lewis Partnership) has been taken from public relations material supplied by the Lewis company, information I have received from friends in England in general confirm the enthusiastic support given the Partnership idea by the workers.

The Andersons, Maumee, Ohio

The Andersons was founded in 1947 by Harold Anderson

as a 500,000 bushel grain elevator in Maumee, Ohio. Today it has branches in three other communities and has developed a large agribusiness operation with annual sales of approximately $750 million. Originally it was a family partnership but in 1973 it began to admit certain employees. Today there are 12 general partners and 155 limited partners. It is, of course, highly unusual for an enterprise of this size to use the partnership rather than the corporate form of business organization. John Anderson, senior partner and son of the founder, explained: "One of the reasons we remain a partnership is that it allows each partner to give away more money—up to 50 percent—and still claim a tax deduction."[9] The maximum contribution a corporation can give is 5 percent.

"This partnership is founded in the belief that all of us are subject to a higher and divine authority, and that we must aspire to goodness, integrity, and those virtues which we discern to be consistent with divine will. We believe that it is those same qualities which entitle the possessor to approval and self esteem, and which further both private and public welfare."[10]

John Anderson outlined the company's "operating set of principles: (1) we believe our company has concurrent responsibilities to our partners, employees, community, and to Christ; (2) our task is to manage our business in the best business manner, with high ethical principles; (3) we believe we have responsibilities to the community besides just giving our time—we donate 20 percent of our profit to community charities; (4) we maintain that 35 percent of our profits should go into profit sharing with employees and partners. For employees this amounts to 50 percent of wages during an average year; (5) we believe that we should guarantee our permanent employees work; (6) we believe that each worker has the right to know the answer to the following questions: (a) what is my job? (b) what does it pay? (c) how am I doing? (d) how can I improve."[11]

Recently the Andersons admitted Ohio State University to the company as a "Community Limited Partner. In this arrangement, charitable institutions receive a donation from the firm which the institution in turn reinvests to become a partner. Thereafter, the new Community Limited Partner shares in the partnership profits." The firm plans to admit two new Community Limited Partners in the next few months, and John Anderson looks forward to expanding greatly this form of partnership in the future. He says, "It is possible that one half of the equity base of the firm could be held by Community Limited Partners within the next 25 to 30 years.... The Community Limited Partnership arrangement provides benefits to all parties concerned—the Community Limited Partner, the Andersons, and the community at large.... The Community Limited Partner enjoys a kind of permanent endowment which will grow as the Andersons grows. The Andersons as a partnership receives a benefit in that additional capital is available for building our physical plant. And this creates expanded job opportunities which, in the long run will be as important to our community's well-being as the income the Community Limited Partner derives."

Anderson says, "There may be other benefits ... of spreading equity widely among many Community Limited Partners. 'Eventually, if things work out as I hope regarding Community Limited Partners, these quasi-public institutions will exert another self-imposed control on our company. They could withdraw their investment if they wanted to. It is my hope that by limiting our power in this way, we can still be motivated by self-interest, while at the same time

enjoy the goodwill of the public, even though we may become a very large company.' "[12]

In an address to students at Goshen College, Mr.
Anderson summarized succinctly points I have discussed at
various places in this book. Capital is needed for the productive process and for providing jobs for workers. This capital
must be owned by someone. He pointed out that one of his
own sons would give away his wealth; others would limit
how much they own. But ownership must rest somewhere—
individuals, charities, or the government. He believes that
joint ownership by individuals and charities is the best arrangement.

Profit Sharing

I have reviewed a number of businesses in England and
the United States which have sought creative new ways of
business ownership. Some of these firms have a form of
profit sharing. I now will discuss profit sharing in a bit more
detail. My comments are based largely on an address given
at the Mennonite Industry and Business Association in 1977
by Bert L. Metzger, a Christian who is president of Profit
Sharing Research Foundation, Evanston, Illinois.[13]

Profit sharing dates from a plan started in Paris, France,
by Jean LeClaire, a Parisian house painter. He "was im-
pressed by a comment of one of his friends that there was no
way to overcome the antagonism which existed between
workmen and master except in 'the participation of the
workman in the profits of the master.' " In 1842 "LeClaire
announced that he would share among his employees a part
of the profits achieved." The idea was greeted with suspicion both by workers and by other business people. But in
1843 he called his 44 workers together and "threw down on
the table before them a bag containing 12,246 gold francs,

and this was labor's share ... labor and management had actually cooperated in producing *incremental wealth*. ... LeClaire distributed this incremental wealth to each worker based on the worker's annual earnings. ... The men returned to their brushes with a new confidence and understanding that if they did a better job and the company prospered, they themselves would benefit directly." This plan is still in existence and "the company grew to be the finest and largest housepainting firm in Paris."

Johann Heinrich Van Thuenen was a German mathematical economist who lived at the time (about 1850) when another German, Karl Marx, was writing his epoch-making criticisms of capitalism. Van Thuenen correctly feared that the Marxist prescription of placing "total economic power in the hands of those with political power would destroy personal freedom." Instead, he said " 'Don't do away with private capital ownership, but rather ... find ways to make everyone a capitalist.' ... Von Thuenen, in addition to being an economist, had large farms in Germany. ... He paid his people a competitive wage rate and then made an agreement with them to share part of the profits of the estate with them. ... He did not pay them in cash. Instead, he invested this money back into the estate in technological equipment and improvements to make the farm more productive. ... He built up individual accounts (for each worker) ... and paid an interest on this principal each year to the workers in cash. After a while the workers were receiving a dual wage—a consumptive wage for their functional activity and an investment wage from their ownership interest in the estate."

John Bates Clark, famous American economist who taught at Columbia University for many years at the close of the nineteenth and beginning of the twentieth century, believed that there were four stages in employer-employee relationships. The first was *competition* "with workers trying to obtain higher wages ... and the employer striving to keep wages low and profits high." The second stage is *arbitration* where an outside third party (often the government) settles the conflict between labor and management. "The third stage is *sharing*, and the fourth is *cooperation*. The only distinction between stages three and four is that sharing takes place in cash in stage three, while in stage four the workers become stockholders as well, and they share both as workers and stockholders."

Ruth Benedict, an anthropologist who had studied many primitive tribes, suggested a concept of synergy. She believed that there are "two kinds of very natural impulses: a selfish impulse (to benefit ourselves by our actions) and an altruistic impulse (to reach out and help the other fellow at some sacrifice to ourselves). . . . Synergy destroys the polarity between selfishness on the one hand and unselfishness on the other. . . . In Ruth Benedict's experience, tribes which organized synergistically thrived. Tribes which did not organize synergistically died—they tore themselves apart." Metzger believes that "profit sharing introduces synergy into the industrial organization."

Some of the pioneering firms in profit sharing in the United States "were Procter and Gamble Co. setting up a sharing program in 1887, Eastman Kodak Co. (1912), Harris Trust and Savings Bank (1916), Sears, Roebuck and Co. (1916), Johnson Wax (1917), and Joselyn Manufacturing and Supply Co. (1918) . . . These few early pioneers were joined by other firms until today there are approximately 300,000 companies sharing their profits with some 14 million employees. The number has been doubling every five years for the last fifteen or twenty years."

I do not propose to give details of profit-sharing plans. Those who are interested should contact the Profit Sharing Council of America, 20 N. Wacker Drive, Chicago, IL 60606. Some plans are cash plans; some are deferred plans; some are a combination of the two. Often they are combined with pension funds or employee stock ownership (ESOP). "Coopers & Lybrand, the big accounting firm, found in a survey of 299 corporate pension plans in five Midwestern states [that] about a third of the companies, most of them medium sized, provided a second plan to employees in addition to the pension plan. Half of the second plans were profit-sharing plans, funded from a set percentage of the employers' profits. The others included employee stock ownership plans and thrift and savings plans."[14]

Are There Other Ways in Which We Can Be Creative?
Throughout this book I have stressed the importance of capital formation and use. It is not possible adequately to provide the necessities of life to the rapidly expanding population of the world unless *all* factors of production are effectively used. It may seem strange, therefore, if near the end of this book I suggest that Christian entrepreneurs experiment with some kinds of labor intensive production.

Let me admit at the outset that entrepreneurs in the United States and Canada are at a competitive disadvantage in labor intensive production. Hourly rates of pay are high. High wages stem from high productivity and high productivity is a result of an extensive use of capital which permits labor-saving productive techniques. Labor costs of production are also high in Western Europe and are becoming high in Japan. Labor intensive production in North America is especially at a real disadvantage when compared with countries like Taiwan, Singapore, South Korea, and especially heavily populated countries like India.

In view of the competitive disadvantage, why should Christian entrepreneurs even consider labor intensive production? There are at least two reasons. In the first place it would provide more jobs. Although labor participation rates in North America are increasing they would go up still more if adequate jobs could be found for unemployed youth—especially minority youth. In other words, we still have a surplus of some kinds of labor. At the same time, our over-use of capital is depleting scarce natural resources, particularly fossil fuels, but other natural resources as well. In the second place, labor intensive production is probably most feasible in small businesses. In such businesses there is a closer relationship between employer and worker, and this provides creative opportunities for Christian entrepreneurs who view their relationships with their employees as a vital part of their Christian calling.

Rates of pay are not high in labor intensive industries. But if the management sets an example of life-style such as suggested in chapter five, and if workers can have a personal sense of accomplishment from their jobs, the actual rate of pay may take on less significance. I am not sure what kind of industries would prove to be the most suitable for this kind of work. Perhaps the production of beautiful, durable, high quality furniture would be an example. I would hope that some Christian entrepreneurs would be willing to risk this or other types of business which, although providing a lower profit margin, would help to bring back to the worker a sense of personal satisfaction *on the job.* Too often this has been lost in highly capitalistic mass production operations. I have confidence that there are many workers who would prefer a sense of accomplishment in meaningful work to high pay in tedious, boring jobs.[15]

A Banker for the Poor

In the 1950s Robert R. Lavelle was one of the few black realtors in Pittsburgh. But he constantly faced the problem of getting mortgage loans for his customers from Dwelling House, a small savings and loan company located in the Hill District, Pittsburgh's largest ghetto. In 1957 he was made a director and secretary of the Dwelling House Savings and Loan. "For several years after, he supported himself, his family, and the struggling savings and loan with what he was able to make in real estate. . . . He was willing to make the sacrifices needed to keep Dwelling House afloat. He had learned, he says, that as a realtor and businessperson he had responsibilities to his community. And they went beyond those normally acknowledged by self-interested entrepreneurs. Dwelling House, Lavelle was convinced, could be an essential (and previously missing) link between the people of the Hill District and something he thought they badly needed—home ownership."[16]

By 1970 "Dwelling House went over $1 million in deposits and was approved for insurance by the Federal Savings and Loan Insurance Corporation. Today, the Hill District's only black-operated savings and loan has over $5 million in 2,500 separate accounts. The bulk of it has been deposited by individuals and groups, black and white, who support Lavelle's explicitly stated policy of 'lending to the greatest need at the lowest possible rate of return.' That policy, however, is a complete reversal of traditional banking norms. 'The system says we're going to lend at the highest rate we can get, at the lowest risk we can take,' Lavelle says. 'That's very prudent economic reasoning. But under that system, black and poor people never get the loan.'

"Lavelle takes a strong personal interest in his customers. He treats those having difficulty with a patience rarely

found in the world of commerce.... But because of
Lavelle's patient encouragement, its foreclosure rate is about
the same as institutions which accept only 'safe loans.' Home
ownership has tripled in the Hill District in the last fifteen
years."

Lavelle's business practices stem from a biblically-inspired
Christian faith. He believes with great conviction that there
can "be such a thing as capitalism with a heart or a soul.
'Make no mistake about it,' he says, 'the capitalistic system is
a system of greed.... [It] is really only concerned about the
bottom line. It doesn't want to consider its moral responsibilities. But it is the only system I have. And besides, the
only way to change something is from within. I know that
Christ came into my heart and changed me. And that's why
I run these businesses now. I want to serve the needs of
people rather than the greed of an institution.'

"Lavelle's personal lifestyle (conservative, but hardly ascetic) and his commitment to home ownership (after all, he
is a realtor) are sometimes criticized. But the fact remains
that ... he has helped improve the material conditions suffered by Pittsburgh's black community, and he has given a
unique Christian witness to an overwhelmingly apostate
business establishment." Are there other Christian bankers
who are willing to take up the same challenge in other needy
communities?

What Lavelle has done for banking in Pittsburgh could
serve as a model for Christian entrepreneurs in other types of
business. I would like to urge that Christian entrepreneurs
direct their skills toward helping the poor of our own countries by seeking to reduce the costs of basic necessities rather
than by producing products for pleasing the already affluent. Furthermore, I think we should have concern for the
poor in the so-called LDCs. This would mean that we would

not engage in business which would exploit Third World peoples or perpetuate income inequities. These inequities are widely recognized as being at the very heart of the failure of Third World development procedures.[17]

CHAPTER 8

Unique Gifts of the Entrepreneur to the Church

Too often in the past we have tended to view the gifts of the Christian entrepreneur too narrowly. In the division of labor within the church we have talked about those who engage in "full-time Christian service" and others who serve primarily by providing the financial resources to support those who are "full-time Christian servants." In chapter six I took the position that the full-time Christian service of the Christian entrepreneur was to engage in work as an entrepreneur in a way befitting one whose prior call is to be a Christian. I also discussed many needs for the financial help business people can give to the church. I made it clear that the Bible teaches that it is the duty of all Christians to give this financial help as they are able.

But the Christian entrepreneur has personal gifts which, though enabling one to earn and to give money, also may be used in other ways in the work of the church. In listing the members of the body of Christ, the Apostle Paul included administrators, helpers, and teachers (1 Cor. 12:28). Christian entrepreneurs have these gifts. This chapter will suggest a few ways in which they can be used in the work of the church.

In the Local Congregation

The local congregation is a fellowship of believers, but it also inevitably embodies certain institutional features. Its mission can be accomplished more effectively if it *organizes* for mission. Typically this means that it will have a board of trustees (or some other group with a different name but a similar function) and a treasurer. Budgets must be prepared. This means that priorities must be established and that each member must be challenged to give. The property of the church must be cared for, utilized as fully as possible (and this will mean multiple use), and kept clean and in good repair. The offerings will be deposited in a bank and checks must be written promptly so that disbursements will meet the needs the congregation has felt called upon to include in its budget.

All of these functions are really *business* functions. In some very large congregations full-time managers are employed to carry out these functions; it is much more usual, however, for some person or persons with business experience to do them as voluntary service to the congregation. This, too, is a Christian service—just as leading the singing, teaching a Sunday school class, or serving as youth leaders.

In the congregation of which I am a member we have a Commission on Stewardship and Administration (formerly referred to as a board of trustees). The change of title was not just a semantic one. Our congregation felt that the group should not only concern itself with the financial resources and gifts of the members of the congregation but with their human resources as well. Just as the Christian entrepreneur, in making daily business judgments mobilizes financial resources for the operation of the business as well as deploys human resources to realize the purposes of the business, so also the congregation must carefully deploy both its financial and its human resources if its purposes are to be realized. This, of course, is a total congregational responsibility in which the pastor(s), the rank and file of members, and the Commission on Stewardship and Administration all take part. But it is a place where the special gifts of those members who have business experience can make a unique contribution.

In the Institutions of the Church

A local congregation, even if it is small, inevitably becomes an institution with certain institutional needs. But many of the broader purposes of the church can hardly be achieved by one congregation working alone and utilizing only its own resources. Certainly this is true in the area of education. Although some individual congregations have established small elementary schools, most schools have a wider base, and this is true of all secondary schools, colleges, and seminaries. In the Mennonite Church alone there are now 74 elementary schools, 14 secondary schools, three colleges, and two seminaries. The largest of these colleges operates on an annual budget of more than $6 million. Some whose personal gifts are in administration are called to serve in the management of the business affairs of these educational institutions. They have often served at lesser salaries than those whose work calls them to private business of similar size. But if the suggestions of this book are followed, this should not result in differing standards of living. There can be only one standard for all members of the Christian community—a *Christian* standard.

Closely related to the educational institutions of the church are those which produce and distribute educational materials. These materials must be written, edited, printed, and sold. The three most basic economic questions any economy faces are: What shall be produced? How shall it be produced? For whom shall it be produced? The Christian entrepreneur faces these questions constantly in making private business decisions. A church publishing house faces precisely the same questions. The Christian entrepreneur will not always allow the market system to operate freely but will, as I pointed out earlier in this book, allow the disciplines of the market to be modified by the demands of a greater loyalty to the disciplines of the Christian faith. This applies equally to a private business or to a church enterprise such as those which provide for the publication and sale of Christian materials. In the Mennonite Church there are now eight Provident Bookstores in the United States and Canada, with six branch outlets. All of them require the services of people with gifts in Christian entrepreneurship.

In a simpler society the task of caring for each other's material needs was usually left to the individual family or the local congregation. This should still be its primary focus. But a churchwide institution such as Mennonite Mutual Aid can serve the family and the local congregation. This is especially true in areas such as providing for hospital and surgical costs, or for providing aid for the survivors in families where loved ones have been called away by premature death or incapacitated by disability. Provision for retirement benefits of church workers involves the accumulation and wise investment of substantial sums of money. Complicated laws concerning income taxes and death and gift taxes make it imperative that specialized counseling be made available to those who want to be sure that their gifts during their lives and the passing of their estate at death fulfill their own commitments to Christian stewardship.

Mennonite Retirement Trust makes possible a systematic way of providing for retirement benefits. Nearly 3,000 church workers participate in this retirement program. Its assets currently are in excess of $6 million. The Mennonite Foundation established a way whereby church members can gain maximum tax advantages from their gifts. Four hundred and fifty participants have contributed to the Foundation. It now has assets of over $17 million. Mennonite Mutual Aid Association is the largest program of all. It provides hospital and surgical aid to over 60,000 adults and children. It has reserves of over $14 million. Private foundations such as the Schowalter Foundation have been established by individual donors who wish to devote their wealth to the work of the church. The management of these and other church institutions requires the services of people with gifts that are very similar to the unique gifts of the Christian entrepreneur in private enterprise.

Various other institutions can be helpful in fulfilling the missionary call of Christ in the Great Commission: a Board of Congregational Ministries, a Board of Education, a general Board of Missions and similar boards on the district conference level, and an overall General Board (Mennonite Church) to coordinate the work of these various church boards and institutions. All of these agencies have budgets and offices to manage and many of them have endowments to invest. The unique gifts of the Christian entrepreneur are called upon to serve these institutions as well as in private enterprise. The Christian principles which guide them should be no different.

In the Boards of the Church

All of the institutions discussed in previous paragraphs have boards which are called to exercise special responsibility in management and in policy determination. In the past many of these boards were composed to a large extent of ordained pastors. This was a natural outcome of the fact that the boards were appointed (or elected) by conference organizations and membership in conference was often composed largely or exclusively of ordained pastors. This was not necessarily a bad idea. The pastors in those days were usually not given financial support by their congregations but, like the tentmaker Paul, earned their own living. Often they were farmers—they were actually Christian entrepreneurs.

Today this is less likely to be the case. Pastors of congregations are persons with special gifts and special training necessary for the exercising of pastoral functions. Such people can certainly render an invaluable service on the boards of the church. But the boards of the church also need persons whose special training and gifts are those of the Christian entrepreneur. Experiences which they have had in applying Christian principles to the operation of their own businesses are making important contributions to the solving of questions with which the boards of the church must wrestle. Essentially these questions are also those of Christian stewardship. As institutions grow they encounter increasingly complex questions of organizational structure. They must solve problems of establishing priorities in the midst of multifarious demands upon limited personal and financial resources. They face questions of salary and wage policies for their employees. Christian entrepreneurs have long wrestled with questions of this sort in the operation of their own businesses. The unique skills they have gained in their experiences in their private businesses can and should be used to serve the larger cause of the church operating through its institutions.

This book has been written in the conviction that God's gift of Christian entrepreneurship is a charismatic gift, not unlike his other gifts to various of his children. "Now there are varieties of gifts, but the same Spirit; and there are varieties of service, but the same Lord; and there are varieties of working, but it is the same God who inspires them all in every one. To each is given the manifestation of the Spirit for the common good.... All these are inspired by one and the same Spirit, who apportions to each one individually as he wills. For just as the body is one and has many members, and all the members of the body, though many, are one body, so it is with Christ.... Now you are the body of Christ and individually members of it. And God has appointed in the church first apostles, second prophets, third teachers, then workers of miracles, then healers, helpers, administrators, speakers in various kinds of tongues" (1 Cor. 12:4-7, 11, 12, 27, 28). Paul likened the members of the church at Corinth with these various gifts to the organs of the human body. "The parts of the body which seem to be weaker are indispensable.... God has so adjusted the body ... that there may be no discord in the body, but that the members may have the same care for one another" (1 Cor. 12:22, 24, 25). It is my prayer that Christian entrepreneurs may recognize their indispensable role in the body of Christ and may use God-given, Spirit-directed gifts for the extension of his kingdom.

Notes

Author's Preface
1. Barbara W. Tuchman, *A Distant Mirror: The Calamitous 14th Century*, New York: Alfred A. Knopf, 1978, p. 37.

2. Miriam Beard, *A History of Business: From Babylon to The Monopolists*, Ann Arbor: University of Michigan Press, 1938, 1962. Although the author, daughter of famous historian Charles A. Beard, was a woman she wrote before a consciousness had developed of sex-bias in references to names of persons. Thus she could entitle her introduction "The Business Man and History." She meant both men and women, just as I do in this book when I use the term businessman.

3. See the interesting article by L. A. King, "Write Your Own Commentary," *Builder*, vol. 28, Oct. 1978, pp. 6-9.

4. Jim Wallis, "The Economy of Christian Fellowship," *Sojourners*, vol. 7, Oct. 1978, p. 4.

Chapter 1
1. Adam Smith, *The Wealth of Nations*, New York: Random House, 1937, 976 pp.

2. The Germans have a similar word, "unternehmer," with the same meaning. The Italian "impresario" also means undertaker but when we use it in English it refers to one who manages or sponsors a musical program or entertainment.

3. For a popular treatment of risk in business see George Gilder, "Prometheus Bound," *Harpers*, Sept. 1978, pp. 35-42. The most significant scholarly treatment of risk is Frank H. Knight, *Risk, Uncertainty, and Profit*, New York: Harper and Row, Torchbook reprint of Knight's classic first published in 1921. Frank H. Knight was for many years professor of economics at the University of Chicago and editor of the *Journal of Political Economy*.

A Mennonite economist, E. Wayne Nafziger, has made several significant studies of entrepreneurship in developing countries. See his *Class, Caste and Entrepreneurship: A Study of Indian Industrialists*, Honolulu: University of Hawaii Press, 1978. Chapter 2 of Nafziger's book (pp. 12-34) gives a concise review of the opinions of various economists concerning the entrepreneurial function: Alfred Marshall, Leon Walras, Joseph A. Schumpeter, Frank Knight, and Maurice Dobb. Nafziger takes the same position I have taken in emphasizing the risk bearing function of the entrepreneur.

4. Frederick B. Tolles, *Meeting House and Counting House: The Quaker Merchants of Colonial Pennsylvania 1682-1783*, New York: W. W. Norton, 1963 (reprint of a book first published by the University of North Carolina Press in 1948).

5. *Ibid.*, pp. 30, 38.

6. *Ibid.*, pp. 49, 59.

7. *Ibid.*, pp. 9, 10.

8. J. Howard Kauffman and Leland Harder, *Anabaptists Four Centuries Later*, Scottdale, Pa., Herald Press, 1975, p. 61.

9. Claus-Peter Clasen, "The Anabaptists in South and Central Germany, Switzerland, and Austria," Goshen, Ind.: The Mennonite Quarterly Review, 1978, pp. 39-47 passim.

10. Leonard Verduin, trans., J. C. Wenger, ed., *The Complete Writings of Menno Simons*, Scottdale, Pa.: Herald Press, 1956, pp. 368-369.

11. Guido Carli and Milton Gilbert, *Why Banks are Unpopular*, Basel, Switzerland: Per Jacobsson Foundation, 1976, p. 1.

12. For recent books which take opposite sides of this controversy see Richard J. Barnet and Ronald E. Müller, *Global Reach, the Power of Multinational Corporations*, New York: Simon and Schuster, 1974; and Raymond Vernon, *Storm over Multinationals*, Cambridge, Mass.: Harvard University Press, 1977.

Chapter 2

1. A. Yemelyanov, "The Agrarian Policy of the Party and Structural Advances in Agriculture," *Problems of Economics*, Mar. 1975, pp. 22-24.

2. *Der Moderne Kapitalismus*, vols. I and II, 1902, vol. III, 1928.

3. *The Interpreter's Dictionary of the Bible*, Vol. III, New York: Ab-

ingdon Press, 1962, pp. 384-385.
    4. *The Politics of Jesus,* Grand Rapids, Mich.: Eerdmans, 1972, p. 36.
See also pp. 64-77. See also Don Blosser, "Jesus at Nazareth: Jubilee and
the Missionary Message (Luke 4:16-30)," *Mission Focus,* vol. VI, May
1978, pp. 5-8, where August Strobel (a German New Testament scholar) is
quoted as having calculated that if the jubilee had been observed
regularly from the time of Ezra, AD 26 would have been the year of jubilee. It was likely that AD 26 was the year of Jesus' ministry in Nazareth.
    5. *Wall Street Journal,* July 20, 1977.
    6. *Ibid.,* July 14, 1977.

Chapter 3
    1. Raymond Baumhart, *An Honest Profit,* New York: Holt, Rinehart
and Winston, 1968, pp. 206-207.
    2. *Ibid.,* p. 5.
    3. David R. Burks, *The Christian Alternative for Business,* Searcy,
Ark.: Harding College, 1977, pp. 175, 180-181.
    4. *Wall Street Journal,* Jan. 15, 1979.
    5. David Ricardo, *Principles of Political Economy and Taxation,* 1817,
p. 90.
    6. *Ibid.,* p. 194.
    7. J. L. Hammond and Barbara Hammond, *The Town Labourer,*
London: Longmans, Green and Co., 1925, p. 149.
    8. *Ibid.,* pp. 173, 175.
    9. R. H. Tawney, *Religion and the Rise of Capitalism,* New York:
Harcourt, Brace, 1926, p. 47.
    10. *Ibid.,* pp. 39-40.
    11. *Ibid.,* pp. 82, 84.
    12. *Ibid.,* p. 76.
    13. *The Complete Writings of Menno Simons,* pp. 647, 651, 658.
    14. Vol. 21, July-Aug. 1978, p. 27.
    15. Emil Brunner; *Justice and the Social Order,* New York and
London: Harper Bros., 1945.
    16. See the comments on the parable of the talents by Donald B.
Kraybill, *The Upside-Down Kingdom,* Scottdale, Pa., and Kitchener,
Ont.: Herald Press, 1978, pp. 138-141.
    17. I acknowledge, with gratitude, my indebtedness to Welby C. Sho-
walter, attorney in Harrisonburg, Va., who offered me these descriptions
of mediation and arbitration when I served as chairman of the Mennonite
Church General Board Task Force on Litigation.
    18. "The Use of the Law," *Assembly Workbook Mennonite Church
General Assembly,* Aug. 11-16, 1979, Waterloo, Ont., pp. 51-56.
    19. *A Statement of Concerns Adopted at a Study Conference on Chris-*

tian Community Relations, July 24-27, 1951, Committee on Industrial Relations of the Mennonite Church, p. 2.

20. *Ibid.*, p. 5. I was a member of the findings committee for that study conference and, if I remember correctly, was the author of the paragraph of the report I have here quoted. I feel as strongly that it is true today as I did when it was written nearly 30 years ago.

21. *New York Times*, May 29, 1977, p. 16.

22. *Wall Street Journal*, Aug. 1, 1978, p. 1.

23. Daniel Kauffman, ed., *Doctrines of the Bible*, Mennonite Publishing House, 1928, p. 454.

Chapter 4

1. *Wall Street Journal*, July 24, 1978.

2. Hedrick Smith, *The Russians*, New York: Ballantine Books, 1976, pp. 93-94.

3. George E. Johnson, "Do Structural Employment and Training Programs Influence Unemployed?" *Challenge*, 22, May/June 1979, pp. 55-58.

4. United States National Center for Health Statistics, *Vital and Health Statistics*, Series 10, No. 80.

5. *Wall Street Journal*, Jan. 24, 1979.

6. *Ibid.* See also the Jan. 25, 1979, issue.

7. Wilbert R. Shenk, Secretary of Overseas Missions of the Mennonite Board of Missions, Elkhart, Ind., and Phil Witmer, Goshen College student who is the son of Robert Witmer, provided me with the description of these workshops.

8. U.S. Law Enforcement Assistance Administration, *National Prisoner Statistics*, Bulletins Nos. 47 and 48.

9. *Wall Street Journal*, July 14, 1978.

10. *Ibid.*, July 20, 1978.

Chapter 5

1. *Federal Reserve Bulletin*, June 1979, pp. A44-A45.

2. This point of view was also expressed by John D. Stahl in an article, "Christian Entrepreneur versus Jubilee," *Weather Vane*, XXIII, May 11, 1979, p. 9. Commenting on my public lectures, "The Christian Entrepreneur," given at Eastern Mennonite College, Stahl expressed the opinion that the profit system itself should be called into question because it "tends to perpetuate injustice." The article was written after the author had heard three lectures and before he had opportunity to read the book.

3. Milovan Djilas, *The New Class: An Analysis of the Communist System,* New York: Praeger, 1957, p. 39.

4. Hedrick Smith, *The Russians*, p. 31. See also pp. 30-67 for details

on the kinds of perquisites enjoyed by this class.

5. Abram Bergson, *The Real National Income of Soviet Russia Since 1928*, Cambridge, Mass.: Harvard University Press, 1961, p. 115.

6. Joint Economic Committee of Congress, *China: A Reassessment of the Economy*, 1975.

7. Martin Hengel, *Property and Riches in the Early Church*, Philadelphia, Pa.: Fortress Press, 1974, p. 27.

8. *The Theory of the Leisure Class*, Boston: Houghton Mifflin Co., 1973.

9. Since women have been so widely accused of being "fashion conscious," I have deliberately chosen my illustrations from men's styles to demonstrate that men, too, are also subject to fashion trends. But if the reader is interested in pursuing the subject of women's fashions, the literature is large and growing. See, e.g., Michael and Ariane Batterberry, *Mirror, Mirror: A Social History of Fashion*, Holt, Rinehart and Winston, for a story of fashion through the history of Western civilization. Ernestine Carter, *The Changing World of Fashion*, G. P. Putnam, provides a history for the twentieth century, prior to about 1960. John T. Molloy, *The Women's Dress for Success Book*, Follett Publishing Co., treats the still more recent period and places its emphasis on "planned obsolescence" in the multibillion dollar fashion business.

10. Ronald J. Sider, *Rich Christians in an Age of Hunger*, Downers Grove, Ill.: InterVarsity Press, 1977, pp. 179, 183. Franz, Kreider and Shelly, *Let My People Choose*, Scottdale, Pa.: Herald Press, 1969, p. 129.

11. Michael Harper, *A New Way of Living*, Plainfield, N. J.: Logos International, 1973. See especially p. 92.

12. *Wall Street Journal*, Jan. 27, 1977.

13. *Ibid.*, July 7, 1977.

14. *Ibid.*, Mar. 23, 1978.

15. Lester R. Brown, *By Bread Alone*, New York: Praeger, 1974, p. 28.

16. *Wall Street Journal*, Mar. 10, 1977.

17. *Ibid.*, Mar. 23, 1977.

18. *Ibid.*, Sept. 22, 1977.

19. *Federal Reserve Bulletin*, July 1979, p. A51.

20. *Wall Street Journal*, Oct. 26, 1977.

21. *Ibid.*, Mar. 4, 1977, Oct. 4, 1978.

22. *Ibid.*, Mar. 24, 1977.

23. Glee Yoder, *Passing on the Gift, The Story of Dan West*, Elgin, Ill.: The Brethren Press, 1978, p. 14.

24. For the struggles of one Christian in determining a Christian standard of living, see Bill Moen, "The Gospel in Stereo: How Can We Be Radical Christians if We Have Good Music Too?" *The Other Side*, vol. 14, December 1978, pp. 49-51.

Chapter 6

1. Arch W. Troelstrup, *Consumer Problems and Personal Finance*, 3d edition, New York: McGraw-Hill, 1965, p. 36.

2. *Ibid.*, pp. 36-37.

3. *Wall Street Journal*, Apr. 8, 1974.

4. *Ibid.*, Aug. 17, 1978.

5. Melvin Gingerich, "Mennonite Income and Giving in 1951," *Gospel Herald*, vol. 46, May 26, 1953, p. 494.

6. Mildred Schrock, "Mennonite Church Giving—1977," *Gospel Herald*, vol. 71, Aug. 8, 1978, pp. 600-601.

7. Sider, *Rich Christians*, pp. 175-178.

8. William E. Keeney, *The Development of Dutch Anabaptist Thought and Practice From 1539-1564*, Nieukoop: B. DeGraff, 1968, p. 135.

9. *Ibid.*, pp. 135-136.

10. J. Winfield Fretz, *The MEDA Experiment*, Waterloo, Ont.: Conrad Press, 1978.

11. Andrew Carnegie, *The Gospel of Wealth*, Cambridge, Mass.: Harvard University Press, 1962, pp. 19, 20, 22, 25.

12. Jan Marczewski, *Crisis in Socialist Planning*, New York: Praeger, 1974, pp. 229-237.

13. *Ibid.*, p. 33.

14. Kenneth Boulding in James D. Smith, ed., *Personal Distribution of Income and Wealth*, New York: National Bureau of Economic Research, 1975, p. 26.

15. John G. Gurley, *China's Economy and the Maoist Strategy*, New York: Monthly Review Press, 1976, p. 292.

16. *Ibid.*, p. 215.

17. This has been stated so clearly in the Focal Pamphlet by Virgil Vogt, *The Christian Calling*, Scottdale, Pa.: Mennonite Publishing House, 1961.

Chapter 7

1. My description is taken from two books by E. F. Schumacher, a British economist who was a director of the Scott Bader Company until his death in 1977. He provides the most detail in his book *Small Is Beautiful, Economics as If People Mattered*, New York: Harper and Row, 1973 (Perennial Library paperback, 1975), pp. 274-292. A shorter statement is contained in *Good Work*, New York: Harper and Row, 1979, pp. 76-82.

2. Schumacher, *Good Work*, pp. 76-77.

3. Schumacher, *Small Is Beautiful*, p. 277.

4. *Ibid.*, p. 279. (Italics in original.)

5. *Ibid.*, p. 281.

6. Quotations are taken from a printed brochure on Bewleys and from a mimeographed document "Change from Private Ownership to Common Ownership in Bewley's Cafes Ltd.," written by Victor E. H. Bewley and dated December 1975. Current information on assets, sales, and numbers of employees came from a letter to me from Miss Rachel Bewley, a member of the Board of Directors. She also explained the project to a group of Goshen College students in Ireland in 1977. Further details may be obtained by writing Bewley's Cafes Ltd., 10 Westmoreland St., Dublin 2, Ireland.

7. *About the John Lewis Partnership,* published by Information Services, John Lewis and Company Limited, Oxford Street, London, 1978, p. 17.

8. *Ibid.,* pp. 17-18.

9. "20% of Net to Charitable Purposes," *Council on Foundations Reporter,* Nov. 1978, p. 9.

10. "A Statement of Principles," The Andersons, Revised 3-77, p. 3.

11. John D. Anderson, "The Christian Businessman", *MIBA Newsletter,* Dec. 1978, pp. 2-3.

12. *Council on Foundations Reporter,* p. 9.

13. Bert L. Metzger, "Sharing Profits with Employees: An Expensive Gift or a Unique Incentive?" *MIBA Newsletter,* Mar. 1978, pp. 1-10.

14. *Wall Street Journal,* March 20, 1979. See also the article by Ezra Byler, "Some Basics and Basic Questions about Profit Sharing," *MIBA Newsletter,* Sept. 1977, pp. 1-5.

15. Hazel Henderson, *Creating Alternative Futures,* New York: Berkley Publishing Co., 1978, *passim*—see especially p. 366.

16. Gary Govert, "If It Comes From God: Profile of a Black Banker Who's Improved the Lives of Hundreds of Poor Families in Pittsburgh," *The Other Side,* June 1979, pp. 50, 52. Quotations in the next paragraph are also taken from this article.

17. Mary Evelyn Jegen and Charles K. Wilber, ed., *Growth with Equity,* Paramus, N.J.: Paulist Press, 1979.

Appendix

A Mutual Fund Which Seeks to Follow Christian Investment Principles

Throughout this book I have assumed that the Christian entrepreneur will invest largely in his own business. After withdrawing from the business enough money to maintain a Christian standard of living (chapter five) and giving generously to charity and the work of the church (chapter six) the remainder will be available for the expansion of the business—an expansion which will provide additional jobs and produce more needed goods or services.

This analysis may appear to neglect the possibility of legitimate investments outside the business. The purpose of such investments might be to diversify risk, to provide for greater liquidity, or to provide for capital gains or for income without at the same time requiring the responsibility involved in day by day monitoring of the investment. These objectives may seem to be especially important to the entrepreneur who is approaching or has already reached retirement.

One usual investment of this type has been the purchase of a home. In the past decade home ownership has also constituted a good hedge against inflation; in fact, home values have advanced more than the general inflation of the price level. Another type of investment which was popular during the 1960s was the purchase of mutual funds—especially mutual funds whose assets were common stocks. But stock funds were not favored during the 1970s; in 1980 some were worth only as much as they were ten years before. Dividend returns have been relatively modest; even by reinvesting dividends they have not kept pace with inflation. The only rapidly growing mutual funds in the past few years have been the money market mutual funds whose assets are short term money market instruments such as Treasury bills of the Federal government and large negotiable certificates of deposits of commercial banks. High interest rates on such securities have enabled money market mutual funds to pay much higher rates of return than the older stock mutual funds.

From the Christian standpoint, another disadvantage of the stock mutual fund is that the stocks which they hold may represent defense industries or industries which profit from the production of gambling equipment or other undesirable things such as alcoholic beverages or tobacco. With the recent renewed governmental emphasis on increasing the defense budget, defense industries may prove to be even more attractive to portfolio managers of mutual stock funds. Christians who have a conscience against using their resources to contribute to such industries might consider investing in the Pax World Fund. This is a fund operated by people who have investment criteria similar to those held by Mennonite Mutual Aid when they purchase stocks for funds which they operate such as Mennonite Retirement Trust and Mennonite Foundation.

A recent article in the *Washington Post* (February 3, 1980) describes this fund and is printed here by permission.

Doves Succeed in Arena with Bears and Bulls
By Martha M. Hamilton

All this and heaven too?

For nine years a mutual fund based in Washington and New Hampshire has been offering investors a chance to earn money through moral investments, earning a decent return for approximately 1,300 persons who have signed up.

"They're not very big, but their performance has been good," said Reg Green, spokesman for a trade association of mutual funds. "They're doing well by doing good. It's not been a dog on the market at all."

The fund is Pax (the Latin word for peace) World Fund, run by two Washington-based Methodist ministers. Pax was started during the war in Vietnam to manage investments for persons who didn't want to put their money into defense-related industries— who wanted to make money, not war.

Since then, according to President Luther E. Tyson and Vice-President J. Elliott Corbett, the fund has overcome initial skepticism and attracted a growing number of investors who earn both modest dividends and growth in the value of their assets.

"In six out of the last eight years we've outperformed the New York Stock Exchange composite, and over the years we've averaged just about in the middle of the mutual funds in terms of performance," said Tyson. At the end of 1978 the fund had net assets of $1.89 million.

In 1979 the fund paid a 57-cent dividend on each share, with the value of a share rising from $8.33 at the beginning of the year to $9.33 at the close, he said. Someone who bought at the beginning of the year and sold at the end of the year could have earned 18.8 percent on the investment, said Tyson.

What distinguishes the fund is what it doesn't invest in—weapons producers, major defense contractors, firms that produce alcohol or tobacco or that run casinos. As social concerns have shifted over the years from war into other areas, the fund also has tried to avoid companies with equal employment problems and is examining new criteria on pollution, said Corbett.

Some of the investment questions are close. "We had a well-known glass company that we brought before our board of directors," said Corbett. "It was a good company with good social practices, but they were the manufacturers of a glass canopy that fit over a fighter plane. We asked our board if that was a weapon."

The decision of the board was not to invest, he said. Also turned down was an elevator company that manufactured simulator training units used to train helicoptor pilots during the war in Vietnam.

"We also have to monitor takeovers," said Tyson. "At one time we were very happy with Montgomery Ward. Then they were taken over by Mobil, one of the 100 largest defense contractors." Other firms such as Holiday Inns and Pan Am have taken themselves out of consideration by a decision to invest in casinos.

Even so, said Corbett, there are enough firms around that a fund can add social criteria to economic criteria and still come out ahead.

Coming out ahead is one of the aims of the fund, but not its chief aim. "The Fund endeavors through its investment objectives to make a contribution to world peace," according to its prospectus.

There are more lucrative investments, Tyson and Corbett concede. "You can get 10 to 12 percent on a money market certificate," said Corbett. "But people invest because they want to be in life-supportive services. They would much rather be in that which builds society up than that which tears it down."

"Right now defense stocks are going crazy," said Corbett. "If you were only interested in making money, you'd be in defense stocks today. But there are a lot of people out there with social consciousness who would rather be in life-supportive investments," he said.

The board of the fund includes Hyman Bookbinder, Washington representative of the American Jewish Committee; Albert D. Boulanger, a lawyer and gerontologist; C. Loyd Bailey, executive director of the U.S. Committee for UNICEF; and Ralph M. Hayward, a retired pharmaceutical company executive. Also on the board are Raymond L. Mannix, a certified public accountant who formerly taught at Boston University, and Henry M. Nevin, an analyst for the United Business Service Co. and chairman of the Civic Unity Committee in Cambridge, Massachusetts. Not all of the board's members are pacifists, said Tyson.

The company's investments are managed by Anthony S. Brown, an investor who manages his own and the fund's portfolio out of an office in Portsmouth, New Hampshire.

The fund has invested in building-product firms, chemical companies, food processors such as Kraftco Corp., retailers, manufacturers and utilities—but no utilities that produce nuclear power.

"We're not in nuclear on economic grounds," said Tyson.

Neither will the fund invest in companies with rocky labor-management relations, "because a company doing business this way will reap the whirlwind," said Tyson, in a metaphor more ministerial than mutual managerial. "Whenever a company has bad labor practices, it's not going to do well over the long term."

Although discussions of whether various types of enterprises are ethical is a constant item of business before the fund's board, the board hasn't questioned the ethics of capitalism, Tyson said.

"We're trying to do the best we can in terms of ethical considerations within the system," said Corbett.

"There is no such thing as 100 percent pure," said Corbett. "Companies have their faults as we do. It's a matter of deciding between better and worse—between not-perfect and horrible."

"When people call us a 'pure' or a 'clean' fund, it drives us up the wall," said Tyson. "It indicates they think we're so unsophisticated we don't know the difference between gray and dark gray."

What the fund has been able to do is demonstrate that people who care can use their influence to create more corporate responsibility, said Tyson and Corbett. Churches and educational institutions also increasingly have adopted social criteria for their investments, they said.

It is an influence in the corporate world that Corbett likened to the Prophet Amos who held up a plumb line to Israel and asked Israel to measure up to it.

General Index

Scripture Index

Carl Kreider has given a lifetime of distinguished service both to the Mennonite Church and to higher education. Best known as professor of economics and business at Goshen (Ind.) College, a position he's held with a few interruptions since 1940, he has also served that institution as dean (1944-70), provost (1971-72), and acting president (1950-51, 1970-71).

His articles on the international commercial policies of the United States have appeared in such journals as the *American Economic Review*, *American Political Science Review*, *Quarterly Journal of Economics*, and *Southern Economic Review*. His books include *The Anglo-American Trade Agreement* (Princeton University Press, 1943), *Helping Developing Countries* (Herald Press, 1968), and *Care for One Another* (Mennonite Publishing House, 1972).

Kreider has served on numerous community, church, and educational committees and boards. He is president of the Oaklawn Psychiatric Center, Elkhart, Indiana, and a member of the Mennonite Church General Board (chairman from 1973 to 1975). He was on the Overseas Committee of the Mennonite Board of Missions from 1961 to 1972 (chairman for four years). Kreider's long-term service on the Committee of Liberal Arts of the North Central Association of Colleges resulted in his appointment in 1974 as an honorary member of the association.

Born in Wadsworth, Ohio, Kreider is currently a resident of Goshen, Indiana. He and his wife, Evelyn (Burkholder), are the parents of four children: Alan, Rebecca (Mrs. Weldon Pries), Stephen, and Thomas. The Kreiders are active members of the Goshen College Mennonite Church.

The Conrad Grebel Lectures

The Conrad Grebel Lectureship was set up in 1950 to make possible an annual study by a Mennonite scholar of some topic of interest and value to the Mennonite Church and to other Christian people. It is administered by the Conrad Grebel Projects Committee appointed by and responsible to the Mennonite Board of Education. The committee appoints the lecturers, approves their subjects, counsels them during their studies, and arranges for the delivery of the lectures at one or more places.

The lectureship is financed by donors who contribute annually $500 each.

Conrad Grebel was an influential leader in the sixteenth-century Swiss Anabaptist movement and is honored as one of the founders of the Mennonite Church.

The lectures are published by Herald Press, Scottdale, Pa. 15683, and Kitchener, Ont. N2G 4M5, as soon as feasible after the delivery of the lectures. The date of publication by Herald Press is indicated by parenthesis.

Lectures thus far delivered are as follows: